Chronicles of Love

Studies in the
Postmodern Theory of Education

Joe L. Kincheloe and Shirley R. Steinberg
General Editors

Vol. 156

PETER LANG
New York · Washington, D.C./Baltimore · Bern
Frankfurt am Main · Berlin · Brussels · Vienna · Oxford

Ana Maria Araújo Freire

Chronicles of Love

My Life with Paulo Freire

Introduction by Donaldo Macedo

Translated by Alex Oliviera

PETER LANG
New York · Washington, D.C./Baltimore · Bern
Frankfurt am Main · Berlin · Brussels · Vienna · Oxford

LIBRARY OF CONGRESS CATALOGING-IN-PUBLICATION DATA

Freire, Ana Maria Araújo.
Chronicles of love: my life with Paulo Freire / by Ana Maria Araújo Freire;
introduction by Donaldo Macedo.
p. cm. — (Counterpoints; vol. 156)
Includes bibliographical references.
1. Freire, Paulo, 1921–1997. 2. Freire, Ana Maria Araújo. 3. Educators—Brazil—
Biography. I. Title. II. Counterpoints (New York, N.Y.); vol. 156.
LB880.F732 F74   370'.92—dc21   00-069650
ISBN 0-8204-5026-X
ISSN 1058-1634

DIE DEUTSCHE BIBLIOTHEK-CIP-EINHEITSAUFNAHME

Freire, Ana Maria Araújo:
Chronicles of love: my life with Paulo Freire / by Ana Maria Araújo Freire;
introduction by Donaldo Macedo. –New York; Washington, D.C./Baltimore;
Bern; Frankfurt am Main; Berlin; Brussels; Vienna; Oxford: Lang.
(Counterpoints; Vol. 156)
ISBN 0-8204-5026-X

Cover design by Lisa Dillon

The paper in this book meets the guidelines for permanence and durability
of the Committee on Production Guidelines for Book Longevity
of the Council of Library Resources.

© 2001 Peter Lang Publishing, Inc., New York

Printed in the United States of America

To Paulo,

for the love lived between us

Nita

Paulo's 75th birthday party at his home in São Paulo, Brazil
September 19, 1996

After losing you,
I am sure to encounter you,
perhaps in the time of tenderness,
where we will say nothing,
nothing happened:
I will just move on,
as enchanted, by your side!

—Chico Buarque

Paulo and Nita in Valencia, Spain
March 26, 1995

Table of Contents

Chronicles of Love

Preface

Coming to terms with pain, with loss is one of the hardest paths a human being can walk. The death of a father, mother, child, or of a great love is not replaceable; no amount of comforting can erase the pain. Each person finds an appropriate corner for his crying, and little by little, the heart stops bleeding. Nonetheless, wounds always remain.

Nita, whom I met alongside Paulo Freire, quickly caught my attention because of the tenderness and companionship with which she treated her husband. I knew the love story he had lived with his first wife, Elza. All our common friends who had been in touch with the couple during exile in Chile, spoke about their most happy matrimony. When I heard that Paulo had married again, and a student, I was surprised and curious. But to be honest, I was a bit disappointed: *How come?! A great love must be preserved forever!*

How foolish to think that way. By observing Paulo and Nita's relationship, I learned that those who live a rewarding relationship, know exactly the meaning and the possibility of such a blessing. They seek, and, if chosen by the Gods, they find. That is what happened to these two partnering souls. There isn't just one half of the orange. For a human being, various are the possibilities for encountering completeness. Paulo accomplished this deed; he had the ability to allow himself to seek and was lucky to find a second and great partner. The complicity in the gazes they exchanged, the tenderness that flowed freely wherever they were, the dedication of each toward the other were a pleasure to see and a complement to the human capacity to live.

When Nita told me about a book "about my and Paulo's everyday life," I realized that she had found a way to bring the pain closer, to embrace it, and little by little, stop the bleeding and just care for the wound. Lya Luft created, out of the pain of losing Hélio Pellegrino, beautiful and difficult poems. There are beautiful paintings and books that are the fruit of this capacity only we humans possess to sublimate loss.

Here, Nita writes, "I intend to quench my longing for Paulo before it immobilizes me." Certainly, this book sets her in motion in the right direction, in the direction of life. But it also affords us, friends and readers enchanted by Paulo, the possibility to live more intimately with him.

No one can be a thinker committed to the oppressed without being deeply in touch with his or her own feeling. I was most touched with a perception, perhaps the simplest, of the book: I am referring to the unknown woman who, with her figure, brought Paulo to realize that he was alive. She did not speak to him, but through her walk, got him to notice desire, the right time to open up the heart to a new love life. Without guilt. Time to open up to the life that still existed. And the unconscious, in its implacable wisdom, gave Nita's image visibility.

Chronicles of Love illuminates the steps taken by Paulo in understanding and coming to terms with the world. It indicates how he—a boy without wide horizons in Recife, with financial difficulties and pain in the home—dealt with the new. It shows how he developed his learning ability, his creativity, and his thinking about what he did not know, the unknown, with which one has no intimacy and that generates fear.

Chronicles of Love is beautiful, profound, and simple, as is all love.

Thank you, Nita, for allowing us to learn a little bit about the intimacy and greatness of one of the most important humanists of this century.

Marta Suplicy

Paulo at 75 years old

Introduction

Chronicles of Love: My Life with Paulo Freire is by far the best window through which to see what it meant for the man who gave the world the classic *Pedagogy of the Oppressed* to be in the world and with the world and with others in the world. In *Chronicles of Love*, Nita Freire provides readers with the opportunity to fully understand Paulo's insistence on viewing history as a constant possibility—a perspective that almost eluded him with the sudden death of his first wife, Elza, in 1986.

After Elza's death, many friends, colleagues, and admirers of Paulo Freire began to see a radical and rapid change in a characteristic that had always marked Paulo and his work: his tremendous idealism. It was the kind of idealism that shields people—even those who are experiencing the worst historical obstacles, social injustice, and discrimination—from losing faith in their capacity as agents of history and from falling prey to cynicism and fatalism. Many of us feared that the death of Elza had cracked the very foundation of this idealism, which had not only attracted us to him and his writings but had also motivated many of us to embrace his challenge to make this world, in his own words, more beautiful, less ugly, more democratic, and less inhumane. Many of us also feared that Paulo had lost his *joie de vivre*, his intense desire to be in the world and to transform the world.

In the winter of 1988, I visited São Paulo to see Paulo, hoping to begin again our collaborative work that had stretched for many years. I remember perfectly the long plane trip from Boston to São Paulo—a trip filled with doubts, fears, and much uncertainty. On the one hand, I wanted desperately to see Paulo and resume our usual conviviality. On the other hand, I was afraid I would no longer find, in Paulo's beautiful and penetrating eyes, the vibrancy that had so marked his ways of being in the world. I did not want to see Paulo without his unyielding belief in utopia as a possibility.

I arrived in São Paulo in the morning and I immediately telephoned Paulo. My initial hesitation disappeared almost completely when Paulo's voice beamed with energy and joy. Even though I was very tired from the twelve-hour trip, Paulo insisted that I come to his house for lunch. As usual, I accepted since it was always difficult to say no to his generous and loving invitations.

When I arrived at his house, Paulo introduced me to a very beautiful—almost classical—woman, who I thought was his colleague at the university. In introducing her to me, he spoke almost passionately about "her fantastic contributions to the Brazilian history of education" and her superb intuition.

When we sat at the table to have lunch I felt a great joy to see Paulo again happy. I noticed his insistence that this attractive, elegant, and eloquent woman sit next to him. During this memorable lunch I realized once again that Paulo always maintained a great coherence between his words, deeds, and ideas. I vividly remembered during that afternoon something that Paulo had shared with me many years earlier: "Never let the child in you die!" His playful gesture toward Nita, his loving smile, his undivided attention while she was explaining her doctoral thesis to us, the frequent gaze, and his almost nervous attempt to hold her hands, made me want to imagine him as a teenager in love.

Many years later, as Paulo and I were walking in New York, we finally talked about the concern that many of us had felt regarding his lack of desire to live after Elza's death.

I told him how happy I was to see him again filled with joy, renewed by an incredible hope, able to dream and love again. I remember clearly when he stopped, and turned slightly toward me, put his hand on my shoulder and said softly: "Yes, Donaldo. I was also fearful that I did not want to live anymore. What Nita gave me was fantastic, magical! She not only made me rediscover the joy of life but she also taught me a great lesson that I intellectually knew but, somehow, I emotionally could no longer remember: to always view and accept history as possibility. It is always possible to love again."

As we walked on Lexington Avenue, Paulo stopped again and said: "Nita not only taught me that it is possible to love again, but she gave me a new and renewed intellectual energy. I feel reenergized intellectually. For example, my new book *Pedagogy of Hope: A Reencounter with* "Pedagogy of the Oppressed" could not have been written without her. She not only gave me new intellectual energy but she also impressed upon me the importance of revising my earlier ideas so as to reinvent them. Her keen understanding of history enabled her to make compelling arguments concerning the importance of rethinking those historical contexts that had radicalized my thinking and that had given birth to *Pedagogy of the Oppressed.* Her important notes to this book and other books that I have written since gave readers an important insight into the historical conditions that made me the thinker, the writer that I am today. This is fantastic! Nita is without a doubt one of the few people who truly and completely understand my work. It is almost scary. Sometimes I think she understands my ideas better than I do."

Chronicles of Love: My Life with Paulo Freire gives readers important glimpses into the type of intimacy Nita shared with Paulo. It was an intimacy without borders or constraints; in it, both of them gave witness to the world as to what it means to love unconditionally, to be vulnerable without fear, to learn from one another, to support each other, and to intellectually commit themselves to an almost quixotic struggle to make this world a more just, less ugly, and more humane place. Nita remains today, by far, the most competent Freirean scholar not only because of the breadth and depth of her penetrating analyses of Paulo's work but also because of her intimate conviviality on a daily and hourly basis. They were almost inseparable: Paulo once told me he missed her even when she had simply gone out to run an errand. It was a conviviality that ranged from soccer matches to the most sophisticated and complex philosophical issues with which they would struggle so as to later share with the world. Because of her complete mastery of Paulo's ideas, Nita is, without a doubt, his heir, even though Paulo himself often said he did not want to leave heirs to carry out his work. He always passionately encouraged and challenged us to reinvent and re-create him. Heir or not, I still strongly would posit that there is no one in the world more equipped than Nita, not only because of her intellectual capacity but also because of her burning passion to reinvent Paulo Freire. Paulo once told me, "Nita made me rediscover myself." From her illuminating notes in several of Paulo's books to the most comprehensive biography of Paulo to date, Nita Freire is certainly the most pointed intellectual to carry Paulo's torch, to create structures that would "make a utopia possible where each one of us, man and woman can be more."

Ironically, Paulo and Nita had crossed paths many years before. That was when Paulo's mother frantically walked the streets of Recife looking (and sometimes begging), for a high school that would give Paulo the opportunity to study for free. Paulo's family had fallen into a deep economic crisis that not only made the continuation of his education impossible but also made him experience "during the greater part of his childhood" the problem of hunger. As he recounted,

> It was a real and concrete hunger that had no specific date of departure. Even though it never reached the rigor of the hunger experienced by some people I know, it was not the hunger experienced by those who undergo a tonsil operation or are dieting. On the contrary, our hunger was of the type that arrives unannounced and unauthorized,

making itself at home without an end in sight. A hunger that, if it was not softened as ours was, would take over our bodies, molding them into angular shapes. Legs, arms and fingers become skinny. Eye sockets become deeper, making the eyes almost disappear.[1]

It was under the circumstance of hunger and the loss of dignity that Paulo's mother walked into Oswaldo Cruz School, owned by Nita's father, and begged for a scholarship for her son. The generosity of Nita's father, Dr. Aluísio Araujo, made it possible for Paulo to continue his high school studies. As Paulo would write about it many years later, his mother

> had left Jaboatão early that morning with the hope that, when she returned in the afternoon, she would bring with her the happiness of having gotten me a scholarship for my high school studies. I still remember her face smiling softly as she told me the news while we walked from the train to our house.[2]

Had it not been for Dr. Aluísio Araujo, Nita's father, it would have been almost impossible for Paulo to continue his studies; perhaps *Pedagogy of the Oppressed* would not have been written. Paulo never forgot his debt

---

[1] Paulo Freire, *Letters to Cristina: Reflections on My Life and Work* (New York: Routledge, 1996), p. 15.

[2] Ibid., p. 63.

to Nita's family and never missed an opportunity to highlight his gratitude for Dr. Aluísio Araujo's generosity.

After he finished his high school studies, Paulo remained at Oswaldo Cruz School as a Portuguese teacher and became Nita's teacher in her early grades. Nita still talks with much emotion of the great admiration she had for Paulo as her Portuguese teacher—an admiration that would turn many decades later into an intense love. It was most certainly the intensity and honesty of their love for each other that motivated Paulo in his last years to dare all of us, "in the full sense of the word, to speak of love without fear of being called ridiculous, mawkish, or unscientific, if not antiscientific."[3]

Nita's presence in Paulo's life not only taught him that to love again is always possible but her presence in his life prevented him from losing what characterized him and his work most: hope. In his last writings, perhaps as a tribute to Nita, he continually returned to the theme of hope, challenging us to embrace it as an essential part of our human condition:

> In truth, from the point of view of the human condition, hope is an essential component and not an intruder. It would be a serious contradiction of what we are if, aware of our unfinishedness, we were not disposed to participate in a

---

[3]   Paulo Freire, *Teachers as Cultural Workers: Letters to those Who Dare Teach* (Boulder, Co.: Westview Press, 1998), p. 3.

constant movement of search, which in its very nature is an expression of hope. Hope is a natural, possible, and necessary impetus in the context of our unfinishedness. Hope is an indispensable seasoning in our human, historical experience. Without it, instead of history we would have determinism. History exists only where time is problematized and not simply a given. A future that is inexorable is a denial of history.[4]

By sharing her life with Paulo with us in *Chronicles of Love*, Nita teaches us the importance of rediscovering the meaning of love and hope. I cannot think of a more fitting tribute to Paulo Freire.

Donaldo Macedo
Distinguished Professor of Liberal Arts and Education
University of Massachusetts, Boston

---

[4]   Ibid.

170 Valença Street

A few days after Paulo's death, our friend Jorge Claudio Ribeiro came to visit me. I told him a number of stories that I had experienced with my husband in travels about the world. As he listened, he showed his grief over Paulo's death, a feeling so painfully shared by so many of us, but especially by me. While embracing my stories—told amid tears and laughter—he allowed me to mourn and to expose the most profound feeling of pain.

Whether with silence, with a laugh, an "umm," or an "oh!" my friend—and he was just as much Paulo's—responded, I realized, with solidarity and sympathy to the pain I was feeling in my entire conscious body.

Each in our own way and in differing degrees of intensity, we cried that afternoon, sitting on the black sofa where Paulo and I had received so many people from around the world, and where a good number of the stories in this book were born—in the living room at 170 Valença Street, São Paulo. We loved that room because it depicted the beauty of our relationship and the joy we derived from building a life together. That was why we had made it, as well as that whole house, beautiful, open, and welcoming. Through that room, in our wordless language, we told those who liked us well just what we were to one another and what we were creating in our shared life as husband and wife, and as intellectuals of kindred ideas who worked in cooperation.

Our common space is gone, but the remembrances of ten years plentifully lived there will never be ripped away or erased from my memory. The things and facts I experienced with Paulo throughout the world, but most of all in that house, I will never forget, because they were lived with loving intensity, with beauty, happiness, and seriousness. Jorge used to talk about the "aura" that cut across that environment. "I leave here in a state of grace," he said as he bid farewell.

Sensitized by what I had heard that afternoon, days later I felt invited to write, to share with all people, some moments lived with Paulo around the "corners of the world," moments drenched in the differences and similarities between us, along with the dissimilarities of many others around the world. I felt motivated to respond to the challenge posed by one of Paulo's publishers, and now mine as well, to put those simple stories on paper, chronicles of our day-to-day love. Differences of culture will appear in many of the stories, not to diminish them, belittle, or deprecate them in any way, but solely to relive times that we had once lived, side by side with love, passion, and friendship. Such times could not be related without a measure of irreverence. In reality, a certain unfamiliarity with different customs on our part comes through, or with behaviors different from the way we were.

I want to relive moments lived with Paulo—on Valença Street and any part of the world—with humor, respect, and longing. Speaking about the apparently simple day-to-day details of our life helps reclaim some of it and shows how much everyday gestures and facts dignify one's relationships with other people and cultures. With these stories I also intend to quench my longing for Paulo before it immobilizes me. This way, whatever life I have from him and with him will continue to live in me. I miss him, but he is—and I want him to be always— present in my life.

Narrating these stories means maintaining this presence, reclaiming my past; it means reliving my reminiscences; it means living my inheritance. By sharing it with you, I am sure it will never diminish, but it will multiply in me. Today I share with you my very own inheritance of the past. It was built with Paulo yesterday.

Sighting on São Luís Avenue

Suddenly, his expression began to change, a sparkle returned to his eyes. He didn't drag his feet as much when walking and took his medication in public less often. He had opted for life once again, after becoming Elza's widower.

This transformation was made to burst forth by a fleeting sighting. While waiting to be helped in a travel agency, where he went to pick up airline tickets to Bolivia, on the *paulistana*[1] São Luís Avenue, Paulo found himself attracted to a woman who walked by on the sidewalk. He clearly realized that his life as a man—and as a thinker—

---

[1] the quality of quintessentially pertaining to the city of São Paulo.

would only have meaning again if lived together with a woman. He observed her as she approached him, as she went by, and as she moved away. He thought about me.

Paulo never knew who she was, but he used to say to me, "That woman was of vital importance. In her discrete walk she 'spoke' to me, without knowing, 'Look, man, you are alive and have the right to live fully.'"

It is not a matter of remaking, but rather making a new, a different life, one that neither substitutes nor continues or denies the previous one. It is a matter of affirming a right marked by difference.

After that incident, he traveled to Cochabamba in March 1987 to accept an honorary doctorate degree from the University of San Simon. He whistled *Explode my Heart*[2] the whole time, I am told by the couple that traveled with him. When asked if he was in love he confirmed it. "Yes, I am, but I can't say with whom!"

Upon his return, in an interview to *Jornal da Unicamp*, he stated his new will to live. He waited until we resumed his orientation of my work on my master's thesis. That was when he proposed that we "change the nature of our relationship."

Obviously, he felt flattered when other women would, in a veiled manner or not, indicate their admiration for him as a man and their desire for more

---

[2]   *Explode Coração* by Gonzaguinha is a popular Brazilian song.

than a great master. But from that day in downtown São Paulo on, he could not wait to say to the candidates, so that their attempts to approach him would not go frustrated, "You know…I have great news: I am in love again!"

To the woman from São Luís Avenue: had it not been for your fleeting appearance, I would not have any of this to tell.

I thank you.

Golden White Slices and Green Beef Liver

In his childhood dietary fantasies, Paulo created certain "mom's recipes." Of course, the foods prepared by mothers are internalized and forever become supreme culinary delights.

In his imprecise and fantastic gustatory reveries, Paulo created two recipes: "golden white slices" and "green beef liver." He insisted on those colors and the corresponding flavors of his imaginary recipes. With a touch of suspicion, at his request, I tried dozens of times to reproduce such delicacies in green and white. I never succeeded.

He sought out witnesses from our region, experts in the local cuisine. Invariably, each would confirm what I had always told him: "Just how can you pan fry slices of bread, soaked in eggs, leaving them white? I don't know; I only know the golden ones! And I've always known beef liver to be brown!"

"This is a plot!" he would reply humorously. "Mom used to make it exactly as I am describing." Once I told him, "With all the respect I have always had for your mother, maybe the only solution is to invoke her spirit in a séance, for only she knows how to make fried eggs look white and beef liver look green without sautéeing it in green herbs!" He used to hate herbs, except for cilantro, which he didn't think worked well for this dish. There was, thus, no possible way to make green liver. He laughed a lot at my suggestion.

On a less psychic note, we decided to phone his sister Stela, who lives in the city of Campos, ES. An excellent cook, she would necessarily be the heir to her mother's recipes. She would certainly be able to clue me in on that family secret. She let out a delicious burst of laughter, appeasing my anxiety. "Nita, I do make them, and mom did too, exactly as you made them. This is all Paulo's dreaming!"

He never gave up these mystical childhood recipes. Even knowing that such feats of culinary acrobatics were impossible, he coherently liked to allow his boy within the sweet dream.

Tom Mix's White Horse

His visits to the movie theater in the Casa Forte district were an essential component of Paulo's memories, especially thanks to Tom Mix movies. Mix was his favorite hero, with his big hat and his white horse. A loyal friend, the horse performed according to its owner's needs. Tom Mix was a cowboy above any suspicion, damsel-in-distress-saving, humiliated-men-protecting, and always ready to take action against injustice.

We went into many a video store in the United States, and after careful and fruitless searches, Paulo would ask the salesclerk, placing his hand on his shoulder, "My friend, have you any Tom Mix movies?"

"Tom who?"

Paulo would insist, as if to force the clerk to recognize such a famous figure, "A cowboy from the old days, from when I was a kid!"

"Sorry, I have never seen or heard about this...what was it again?"

He would pretend to forget that disappointment and, at the first opportunity, he would go into another store and repeat the question, and get the same response. One day, at my daughter-in-law's sister's house, a large, remodeled townhouse in Greenwich Village, in New York, the conversation shifted toward today's children's love of "action movies." The memory of Tom Mix came to Paulo very strongly, and, quite unbecoming of him, he dared to ask, "Cari, do you think your husband (Matthew Modine) could find a Tom Mix movie in one of those Hollywood studios? I need to see at least one of them again!"

"We'll do what we can."

Cari said that with a tone of commitment. More than a year later, we returned to New York. We stayed at my son Eduardo's house. There it was, a tape, an awaited gift. We immediately put it in the VCR. Stunned, Paulo realized the gap between his childhood images and the reality in motion right there.

"Nita, how could I have thought all my life that Tom Mix's horse was white? In *Letters to Cristina* I wrote that, and that I used to go with Temístocles[1] to see Tom Mix's full-length movies!"

He was perplexed. It was a hard blow to realize that the horse was not white. Only the hero's huge hat was white. Upon our return to Brazil, he suggested that we watch the tape again.

"My goodness! Dudu's[2] brother-in-law went through all this trouble, researching, asking, buying this tape! This is not possible…the horse was white, and his movies were not just these short episodes."

His boyish side, which he never lost, was inconsolable. Finally he concluded, "Nita, I'd rather hold onto the Tom Mix from my childhood, riding a beautiful, elegant white horse!"

---

[1]   Paulo's brother.

[2]   Nita's son.

Child's Dream

So many times, as we held hands or caressed each other, Paulo would talk about his childhood dreams, whether realized or frustrated, naive or possible:

▶ *Visiting London:* to that boy, the British capital had the flavor of everything one could desire. He had read that that was where all good and important things in the "civilized world" happened, and that it had nothing to do with his Recife. In Recife, the "English of Apicucos," isolated themselves from the "underdeveloped Recifeans," while enjoying all the best in life, including telephones, electricity, and train and streetcar services.

Paulo visited London as an adult. But the one in his dreams was different. The actual city was much too concrete, and it was alarmingly different from Recife. It was not the city of angels and gods.

▶ *Digging an enormous tunnel,* from Recife to Tokyo or Osaka, either one. What mattered was getting to Japan, a surprising nation not only because of the eyes and skin color of its people, but also because of its traditions of red dragons and giant Buddhas. If, when he punctured the globe in his classroom, the pointy object would come out on the spot where the Land of the Rising Sun was drawn, why not dig a real tunnel? This dream lasted up until he became aware of what a child's curiosity is capable of.

▶ *Having a pair of sneakers,* which, back in his day, in no way resembled the ones available today. Rubber soles and white canvas, with dingy laces. He got a pair from his parents and wore them day and night. He would go to sleep with the sneakers in bed or with them on. He never forgot that day.

▶ *Owning a bicycle.* He never rode on one in his lifetime. In 1988, we spent fifteen days at the University of California, Irvine and I encouraged him to learn how to ride then. I would ride around the campus, and he would look on admiringly and with a bit of harmless envy. We even went as far as to look for a padded jacket in a store, but we realized that nothing could protect him from a fall, a distinct possibility. Having discarded imprudence, he had to be content watching me slide through the tree-lined lanes of the beautiful university, which was, incidentally, designed by a Brazilian. His eyes, however, contained a degree of frustration.

▶ *Becoming a priest:* under the influence of his mother, a woman guided by faith and religion, he briefly nourished this possibility. He gave it up upon finding out that priests don't get married. Paulo was slow in starting to speak. He did not talk much until he reached the age of five or six. He used to tell his mother that he would only talk when he knew well what to say and how to say it. Once he learned, he liked to talk and talk. He truly disliked being alone, needing attention and tenderness. How, then, could he be celibate? A wise decision, even if made at a tender age.

▶ He patiently waited for almost seventy years for *the gift of a soccer ball.* This one was among his most hidden desires. When I finally realized it, I got him one as a present for Christmas in 1995. A ball, one of the good leather ones. He was very happy when I guessed his wish, for his poor childhood never offered more than balls made from socks to play in the fields of Recife or Jaboatão.

► *Witnessing the turn of the century and the millennium:* "A harmless dream, characteristic of anyone wanting to live a long life," he used to say. A mystical, tellurian dream? Perhaps. It contained an element of the unexplained, but also of his utopia of witnessing better days.

So many childhood dreams, possible or not, realized or not, are still out there, waiting to be nourished and made concrete by us.

Young Man's Passions

In our conversations, Paulo liked to remember the passions of his youth. He first fell in love when he was about fourteen years old. It was one of the women who washed clothes in the Jaboatão River, worn out by her heavy labor, who would lustfully gaze at the teenagers who swam around there.

This was a woman in her forties who liked to initiate young men into their love life. Paulo decided to go to her house. Provoked by her libidinous gazes and by friends' descriptions of how she would contort herself in bed, Paulo fearfully left for his rite of initiation. However, before things had even gotten started, he was running fearfully out of the two-room shack where she lived with her husband. He went to confession with the parish priest.

/ /

A few years later, in Jaboatão, Paulo fell in love with the daughter of the richest businessman in town. This family lived in a big, old colonial house in the center of town; the home was very beautiful, painted blue, with large louver windows where the wind would blow through the ferns hanging on the porch. It still stands today.

A few times, she disobeyed her parents' prohibition to meet with him. It was a mutual but impossible passion, because of the social class difference reinforced between them by the fear of an exemplary beating, usually dispensed to her more daring suitors. As always, a zealous father tried to keep his daughter away from a love that was in his view misguided. Paulo suffered, but before her father interfered in such violent manner, he decided to keep away from that "beautiful girl: long shiny hair, vivacious eyes, slim figure, sensuous lips, fine and rosy skin on her face."

/ / /

Still prepubescent, he also fell in love with a young woman who lived in the São José district in Recife. Every afternoon, while resting her arms on a red pillow with huge flowers printed on it, she enjoyed leaning over the windowsill to watch all the activity on the street. She took advantage of that position and the generous necklines in her showy dresses to set herself apart from the other young women on the street, who displayed themselves in similar fashion.

As a daily excuse to witness her unabashed exhibition of sensuality, every afternoon he would visit a classmate from the Oswaldo Cruz School who lived next door to her. One day he decided to declare his feelings. He stopped in front of the window, looked at her with desire, and, intending to initiate a relationship through conversation that seemed gentlemanly to him, he said daringly, "I walk by here every day to see you, because I think you are beautiful!" While moving her body sensuously, she replied with slight disdain, "All the boys who walk by here tell me that! Thank you so much!"

He never walked along that street again.

iv

That humiliation having passed, Paulo fell in love with a young woman who took the same train as he did every day between Jaboatão and Recife. After a few days of reciprocal eye contact, they started sitting next to each other. Then, they would travel amid more and more ardent kisses and embraces. After getting off at Central Station, they would walk arm in arm all the way to the Our Lady of Carmo School, where she studied; he would go on to the Oswaldo Cruz School, at 1013 Dom Bosco Street. At the end of classes, they resumed their exchanges on the way home.

They used to love it, he would recall with some enthusiasm, when it rained. With their clothes soaked, they would seek refuge under marquees or hidden corners, and they would take advantage of the situation to press their bodies together and kiss each other more intimately and voluptuously. Winter break interrupted their passion. After mutual vows of eternal love, she traveled to Caruaru, and he went to Belo Jardim.

The vacations went by. On the eve of his return to Recife, a friend told him that he had seen his beloved enraptured in love with a rich young man from Caruaru. Paulo said nothing to the bearer of disillusionment. He went to see her. He asked if what he had heard was true. She denied it. They argued. He listened to his friend and locked himself in his room for three days, neither eating nor talking. His mother's pleading did no good. He only came out when he felt cured from that great and last pain from unrequited love. He forgot it forever.

The "Taxi-Girl" from Maciel Pinheiro Square

Like all teenagers in the early 40s, Paulo dreamed of dancing the bolero, blues, swing, samba, fox-trot, and tango. He did not want to run the risk of making a fool of himself when asking a nice girl to dance at a party. He learned that there were special places just for dancing; there, the *bambas*, "expert male dancers," enjoyed having equally competent partners while moving their bodies around the dance floor. Beginners would seek help there as well in taking their first steps. Armed with courage, he left after finishing some chores at the Oswaldo Cruz School and marched, under the shade of large ficus trees, all the way to Chora Menino Square. At that point, he took Manoel Borba Avenue and proceeded to Maciel Pinheiro Square.

Along the way he kept popping the seeds from the trees—small, firm balls that made a characteristic "pop" when stepped on—that children and teenagers liked to play with. Paulo anticipated the pleasure he would experience while gliding smoothly around the dance floor.

When he got to the square, with its white marble benches, he gazed at the birdbath that adorned it. He was careful not to be seen by any acquaintance that might walk by. He identified the entryway to the dancing studio and went upstairs. It was three o'clock in the afternoon; it was hot, and there he was in a white suit and necktie in a ballroom surrounded by *taxi-girls*.

He bought a card that entitled him to dance to twenty songs. By his calculations, the price fit his meager income from private tutoring. He was sure it would be worth it. He looked around. "How deplorable; young women of all physical types, poor ones, sitting down, waiting for someone to pick them. But, what would they be doing were it not for his humble labor?" he thought. Loud music pounded out through the open windows. Paulo perspired, more from fear than from the heat. As he looked around at the girls, he was fixed on one. "This one will be patient with me…she looks like she can handle it if I step on her foot!" he pondered. He took a deep breath and, fixing his gaze just on her so as not to give the others false hope, he addressed her. "Can you teach me how to dance?"

The young woman stood up and opened the little wooden gate that separated the dance floor from the waiting area for him. She waited for him to take her in his arms. She realized that this would indeed be his first class. "Put your left hand in my right hand and your right hand around my waist; I'll settle in by resting my left hand around your neck," she instructed.

He managed to position himself correctly. The music began. Leading with her own body, she whispered, "Two steps to the right, one to the left…two there, one here …come on, come on, smile…relax, listen to the music, feel the rhythm…don't be afraid, go on, you'll learn, it's easy, it feels good…move your body, follow me more firmly, but leave me free…it's good to shake your body!"

When he told me this story, Paulo would make a point of saying, "I was not wrong in choosing that young woman. She was great, encouraging me as much as possible. She was pretty, friendly, and competent. Not once did she complain that I kept stepping on her feet. Not at all! All her talking was personable and tender. No censorship."

The student, however, was not very excited and quit in the middle of the lesson. He said good-bye to his teacher hurriedly, "Thank you so much. You are an excellent professional, very friendly, but I am a hopeless case! Sorry I stepped on your foot so many times!"

He ran downstairs, and she followed, "Sir, you have only danced one song; you still have nineteen left! Another rhythm is just about to begin; let's try it...come on, don't give up!" Intent on freeing himself from that situation where he felt uneasy, he said, without looking back, "Sell the card to another customer; keep all the money. This is a good chance to make some extra. Thank you very much! Thanks for the lesson!"

Singer's Calling

Once, on the black couch of our living room on Valença Street, Paulo told me that when he was a teenager he sometimes felt the urge to become a singer. For several years he would get together with some friends on Sunday afternoons, back in the Jaboatão days, for vocal sessions. They would simulate an auditorium, the stage, the MC, the audience, the microphone, and everything they supposed was necessary for a radio program.

One day, a more daring member of the group decided to sign up for a real program, at the Pernambuco Club radio station. On the set day, there was our anxious contestant in bed, sick with a cold, a fever, and a hoarse throat. Paulo made the trip to the capital and took his friend's place. Everyone in the group knew all the songs,

— ♪♪ —

and there was no rehearsal for amateur hour. One could pass for the other without any problem.

Young Paulo's extreme shyness was concealed behind the friend's name, and he managed to let his voice be heard. Applause and a cash prize later, the whole group was waiting for his return at the train station. They had listened to his success through an old tube radio that picked up more static than music, but that they all avidly clung to nonetheless.

Paulo mustered some courage and, months later, signed up for the same program, this time under his own name. He got there, started singing, and got into it. He was fearless and happy. But, a few seconds later, the gong sounded, indicating that his performance was over. "My doubts about whether to be a singer or a Portuguese language teacher are resolved. I'll stick to teaching syntax and singing just for the family," he decided right then.

The years went by. On the day he turned fifty, he was convinced that he still was an OK, if not great singer. He saw his adolescent dream crumble once and for all at a little birthday party in Geneva. When he had proudly given his guests his "official gift," a cassette recording of his singing in the style of Silvio Caldas, Chico Alves, Nelson Gonçalves, Orlando Silva, and other vocal giants of that era, someone said, "ridiculous." That was all it took for him to abandon, in one fell swoop, his calling, first heard in

Jaboatão. I never heard him sing again, but judging from the famous recording, I found his voice to be excellent.

He then took up whistling, which he did very well. He enjoyed both popular and classical music: Villa Lobos, Vivaldi, and Mozart. He would whistle in moments of tenderness with me, showing his musical, boyish side. Firm and thick lips pressed forward, full cheeks, he would concentrate, attune himself, and then begin, going for minutes on end. He complained that his lungs, filled with nicotine, did not help much any more. Sometimes, in moments of anger or extreme worry, his whistling was a way to ease his discomfort. It was his catharsis. While whistling, he would hide behind a door and I would try to find him. When he came home, his whistle from a distance was a tender sign that it was indeed he who had come in. I always took great delight in this habit, which he loved, and that provided us with so many moments of happiness. So many times he declared his love for me in this way: simply whistling!

Deeply, Remembrances

Paulo enjoyed telling me passages, whether happy or melancholy, from his entire life. He remembered his father ill at home, the family living on Enchantment Road in Recife and, from 1932 on, in Jaboatão, ironically, on Health Hill. He would speak about his mother, about Aunt Lourdes, about his grandmother, his brothers, his Aunt Ester and cousins Dosa and João, who had also gone into "exile," eighteen kilometers from the capital.

He used to talk a lot about Uncle Lutgardes, whom he admired a great deal. His uncle, along with his wife Natércia, had waited for him at the airport on Governador Island in the middle of so many Rio nights, and hosted him at their house in Urca. A nice house, friendly conversation, new ideas, typical of the National Capital. He would see his cousins, Leda, Stênio, and Naná, who had advanced customs that he had a hard time accepting. He would listen and elaborate, and almost always see that they were right. With them he learned how to draw different readings from the world.

He would recall Uncle Rodovalho, the poet, bohemian, ladies' man, and tradesman. He had gotten rich in the '20s in Rio de Janeiro, and he would religiously send his mother—Paulo's grandma who lived with them—a handsome allowance that helped support the entire family comfortably. Not satisfied, from time to time he would ship them boxes of imported fruit, much to the family's delight.

Rodovalho's business went bankrupt with the New York stock market crash, and the whole family went down with it, both his in Rio and Paulo's in Recife. That was the reason for their move to Jaboatão. Paulo went to visit him a few times in the '40s, in São Paulo, where he had fled to escape the ruin he had fallen into in Rio. Later, enriched once again, and in love with a woman who would leave him at the first sign of a new financial fall, he fell into a sorrow from which he never escaped. He ended up dying from illness and from nostalgia over his financial and personal losses, above all that of this woman. Many years later, Paulo received from his wife a book of poems written by his uncle. We even read some of the poems together; some very beautiful. They spoke of his pain.

"A magical solution it was, to think that by fleeing Recife, we would be able to remain middle class a few kilometers down the road," Paulo used to say. He mentioned that his Aunt Lourdes used to protect her eldest nephew, his brother Armando, by giving only him a few dollars, by giving him better food, and even by doing some of his homework.

This situation encouraged solidarity between the "less favored," Paulo and his brother Temístocles. Without the aunt's protection and without money to buy treats, they fended for themselves by stealing fruit and chickens from around the neighborhood. Soon they had made a new friend, Dino, who joined them to eat the freshly picked fruits from other people's backyards. They would give the chickens to their mother, already a widow then, who would prepare them, with shame and discomfort, to feed the hungry family.

/ /

In the summer of 1996–97, we were invited to a Pernambucan supper at the home of a family who came together to see Paulo again after decades of separation, and also to meet me.

We savored delicacies made with sophistication—couscous in coconut milk, pamonha[1], canjica, casava cake, casava and corn couscous, tapioca with grated coconut, Souza Leão cake, and peanut brittle. Then we went out onto the tropical verandah swept by a fresh breeze and took a nostalgic trip all the way back to the Jaboatão of river swimming, provocative women doing their wash, the trips on the steam locomotives, and the poverty of friends having a hard time finding schools. We recalled Mr. Armada's haunting ghosts[2], and the phenomenal beating a "zealous father" had given a city boy for having violated his daughter.

When we left, Paulo observed, "They remembered everything, except that Temístocles and I were the most regular visitors to their backyard. Undesirable guests who would run away at the first warning holler, 'Get them! These kids are stealing!' The parents of these people who welcomed us so hospitably never kept the threat. They certainly cultivated a spirit of understanding and forgiveness, to the point that they didn't make the slightest mention of our 'sneaky visits.'"

---

[1] a corn-based meal cooked in corn husks similar to the Mexican tamale.

[2] ghost stories told to Paulo when he was a child.

/ / /

Paulo used to recall, with melancholy, the dialogues he would hear between his parents when he was about ten years old, after they lost Uncle Rodovalho's financial support. The house where they lived in Recife also belonging to his uncle, had no ceilings, and the walls did not go all the way to the roof, so one could hear in one room what was said in another.

On those nights when he was afraid of ghosts who might come to get him or to touch his feet (as he used to imagine) with their nasal voices and terrifying fingers, the boy would quietly listen to discussions about the family's problems. His parents would keep their voices low when talking about their poverty. They would evaluate the options for augmenting the family's meager budget, especially since his father had been given early medical retirement.

With sadness, Paulo would tell me about the solution they found: his father was going to travel to the interior to buy items they could sell in Recife. They made a deal with the owner of the convenience store on the corner. The boy would see his father leave on the train and would imagine him doing business, on donkey back, out in the country, dealing in pots and pans, clay figures, caruá rope, straw baskets, and sun-cured meat. The profit was too small for a man removed from the post of lieutenant with the military police for health reasons. Being pressed against a wall by a horse while on the job had injured him.

In the whispering of those sleepless nights, worsened by the lack of success in their initial venture, the couple thought they had found a new way to deliverance: the brown sugar business. Once again the boy's father left, this time on a shorter journey to the forest zone of the sugar-producing region. Days after, he returned, full of merchandise and hope. Once in a while, his father would go to the store to see if any money would trickle in, but disappointed, he would watch the heap go untouched.

The boy would secretly engage in the same routine, and quietly suffer his father's failure. He knew that displaying solidarity at those times would be like uncovering a secret his father would never reveal. He respected him that way, and, as an adult, continued to do so. He did that for so many people. "What could they have done in that Brazil of the '30s? Nothing! Failure swept all who did not belong to the political-economic elite. We have improved a great deal since, but my father could only have done what he did," he used to say, indicating that he understood the limits imposed by the circumstances.

Ironically, his parents' broken dreams nourished the adult Paulo's capacity to think, to act, and to make decisions. And to do so without sectarianism, without hate or vengeance, but rather with creativity, daring, and thoughtfulness. He knew his father was one of the many "pilgrims of possibility" who did not succeed, but enabled him to become a "pilgrim of the obvious" who worked out.

IV

Two other situations hurt Paulo a lot. They involved his mother, Dona Tudinha, whom he liked to speak about as a tender and intelligent woman who cared a great deal for her children.

First, he regretted the "implicit prohibition" imposed on his mother by her children concerning remarrying. Widowed at forty-two, she never married again. Given the choice of being happy and her children's wish, she opted for the second alternative. "I was selfish, a macho adolescent who did not encourage his mother to find new love. Today I can see how wrong I was. It is a tyranny for children to want their parents all to themselves, not caring about their life options. Children often fail to respect parents' legitimate decisions for a new romantic and sexual life," he always repeated.

He could see her interest in the mail carrier, younger than she was. But that was not the determining factor. Suffering, but without guilt, he would add, "We were not able to understand that they loved each other and were entitled to happiness. Back in those prejudiced '30s, she was a victim of our absurd reading of the world regarding the right to life."

He talked about his mother's tremendous effort to take care of her kids after her husband died. She would buy on credit at the grocery, do embroidering for rich brides, or accept stolen chickens the children would bring home. So many times, the boy went to the grocery with his mother's list only to bring back this rude message: "I'm not giving you anything! Only when she pays me what she already owes me. I have provided kerosene, cured meat, and flour, but I have yet to see any money." He also suffered when he remembered how the rich women would devalue his mother's precious embroidering by bargaining for a better price, and she would give in to avoid losing a customer.

I met Dona Tudinha shortly before her death in the '70s. Her expression contained the dignity of a woman who, in spite of much suffering, believed in her victory as a widow and a mother. On the black couch in our living room, holding hands, I heard from him these stories about his family. I would listen to him in silence. "When I die, write about these things that lack of time or sadness preclude me from telling," he asked me numerous times.

He would recall his mother's first visit to the army base in Olinda, where Paulo was arrested after the military coup[3] in 1964. Innocently, she told the captain who had brought her boy there, "Mr. Captain, my son is very good, serious, and generous, and he does not deserve to be incarcerated here." To which Paulo replied, "I do need to be here, Mom. If this right wing coup had spared me, it would have been a sign that I am not, as I am and wish to be, for the oppressed and exploited. It would have been a certificate that I had preached one thing and practiced another."

The second situation that hurt him a lot was not having been able to provide his mother the opportunity to go meet with him in exile. Not having seen her after 1964 caused him to suffer so much that, whenever the subject came up, he could not go on. While in exile, especially during the Medici administration, Paulo would send letters to his mother through two, sometimes three intermediaries. Someone in the World Council of Churches would take the letters out of Switzerland and address them to a person in Brazil who would then send it to some progressive priest who would then mail it. A simple letter from a longing son to the mother who loved him so seemed to travel such a tortuous route! The reply would follow the same path in reverse, not to spare him more inquests for "acts damaging to the nation," but persecution in exile.

---

[3]   A military coup against President João Goulart that established a dictatorship that lasted until 1979.

Paulo would remember these facts without blaming himself and without pointing fingers. He anguished. He understood that such a state of affairs had been produced by life's circumstances, by a society with aristocratic and prejudiced structures, and by a feeble and unjust state. Dialectically, he forged himself to denounce it.

Permanently imprinted in his memory was his mother's pilgrimage in search of a school and her meeting with my father, who granted her a scholarship for the six years of secondary school. I saw him for the first time before I turned four. In his most passionate declarations to me, he would say that such a precocious encounter "had not happened by chance, but so that I could meet you and, many years later, encounter you again, deeply, truly, and passionately." During these talks, his eyes would sparkle. "Don't you remember, Nita, we met each other in ancient Greece. I learned the epistemological dialogue from old Socrates, and you participated too!"

I loved such a great declaration of passion, and I lived, in other ways, the same ecstasy that bonded us, although sometimes I provoked him with my sense of reality, bringing us down from wonderful lovers' dream. "Paulo, I don't think I could have sat on this bench of the Agora in Athens. Women could not debate with philosophers!" I observed to him.

"Yes, you could too! In a dream everything can happen!"

It is true. In the game of love everything can happen!

The Jailer's Flings

We were having lunch on a Saturday, at a modest restaurant in Maceió, along with the Secretary of Health and an educator who had organized a conference on adult education. We had just returned from Deodoro, the old capital, whose beauty thrilled me. I admired the Brazilian creativity in churches, with all their gold, wooden carvings, pulpits, altars, and baroque statues, in the stones that formed the walls, and the large roof tiles sheltering it all.

Our hosts had chose the restaurant. At Paulo's insistence we have goat tripe, a typical dish from the

Northeast, which is said to have been Lampião's[1] men's favorite. With his gentle manner and a smile, the secretary stated, "Professor, a friend of mine will be joining us for lunch who met you in 1964. He was your jailer at the base in Olinda."

I was startled. My husband, on the other hand, tame and opensouled, just asked, "What is his name?" The officer's name did not ring any bells. When he arrived, Paulo did not recognize him. He touched the man lovingly on the shoulder and asked, "Son, tell me some stories from the time that we lived back at the base so that I can identify you."

He was the officer who had taught the political prisoners a few strategies to manage to get out of the cubicles where they were confined so as to preserve their health.

"I would say, 'Ask for water, ask to use the bathroom, move your body or you will not survive,'" he said.

"Are you a general yet?"

"No, Professor, I have been on reserve since the '70s. Back in those days, I went to arrest another professor. Picture a horrible situation. My eyes fell upon the daughter of the man I handcuffed, and hers fell upon me.

---

[1] An outlaw-hero who lived in the Brazilian Northeast and who had a legendary and romantic reputation of daring, resistance, and perversity against the establishment.

A spark was exchanged. It was love at first sight! It was tough. I watched the father by day and loved the daughter by night. We loved each other a lot. But one day, the general called me in and asked, 'Lieutenant, is it true you are a traitor to our nation?' Standing at attention, I denied it three times. Then, he asked the fatal question, 'Is it true you are having a fling with the daughter of a traitor arrested in one of our bases?' I could not deny my love. I chose to say, 'Yes!' I reckoned my punishment would be smaller!"

We were terribly curious to find out what had happened to him.

"Then, the general shouted, in an upset voice 'Lieutenant, tomorrow morning, at six A.M., you, sir, are leaving for the Amazon. You are hereby transferred.' All that was left for me to say, once again, was, 'Yes, my general.' I knocked my right foot against the side of my left foot, and saluted him as any military officer would in bidding their superior farewell. I spent ten years at a place four hundred kilometers from Manaus. There, little by little, I understood that the 'Redeeming Revolution' had been a coup, and that it had been a good thing to treat the prisoners with dignity. I went on reserve."

My Cupid did not allow the lieutenant to go on with his story. In a demonstration of his love for life, and for the act of loving itself, rather than an interest in scrutinizing the hard times of injustice that man had witnessed, he asked, "Tell me, after all, did you marry that young woman?"

"No, Professor, the forest, the distance, and the lack of communication separated us forever!"

Small Habits

Paulo had many habits that revealed a little of his enchanting personality. Every morning, he would get out of bed to take a long shower with very hot water. "I finish waking up in the shower," he would say. At breakfast, he would come into the kitchen with his medication for the day in hand. He would place it in a small container. He would then have fruit, sometimes eggs, bread, and black coffee. At the end he would religiously take the medications to control his blood pressure.

If I were in my office when he got up, he would call me on the intercom, "Love, I am going to have breakfast; what are you doing?"

I would come up the circular staircase and join him in the kitchen since his question meant, "come be with me."

We would kiss. We talked to the young woman who worked for us, "Helena, did you see the soap opera yesterday? What happened?"

More than out of curiosity, he would ask this question to involve her in our day-to-day lives. She would tell everything, down to the smallest detail. It was as if we had seen the previous night's episode. We would read the papers on the sunny verandah, while listening to classical music on the Cultura radio station or from CDs I would select for our enjoyment: Vivaldi, Mozart, Bach, Beethoven. We would discuss the news of the day and then go downstairs to our offices, which were adjacent to each other. He would read books or reread some work of his own in progress before resuming writing. He would do everything by hand. The electronic equipment in our office awed him, but he left the use of it all to me and to our secretary.

He always had lunch at home. Even when he was working outside of the house, he would come for his "homemade food"—beans, rice, meat, fruits, sweets, and juices. Depending on the dish of the day, we would have the red wine of his choice, Spanish Rioja or a French Beaujolais. His frequent aperitif was a glass of Brazilian Cachaça. He was not fond of vegetables, except those in the famous stew.[1]

---

[1]   A Brazilian dish prepared with meat and several vegetables.

Chronicles of Love

In the afternoon he would again work. He was always involved with writing, giving interviews to magazines, teachers, students, researchers, or journalists from around the world. On some days, he would teach his classes at PUC-SP[2], and UNICAMP[3], and continued to do so until 1991, when he terminated his affiliation with the institution.

When he was tired, he would ask to go for a car ride. I would drive, and he would sit by my side and put his hand in mine, either talking or simply watching the countryside.

During the frequent times that we traveled abroad, we would work a lot by day, but whenever possible, I would seduce him into dating by night. Thus, we attended ballets in New York and Flamenco dances in Madrid. We applauded several performances on Broadway and in Paris. I am happy that it was with me that he had those moments, since before me he did not allow himself that right.

A few times we went to the movies or to the theater in São Paulo. We used to enjoy staying home, talking just by ourselves or with friends. Sometimes we just watched TV. Always close together, holding hands, caressing each other. According to Heliana, my daughter, if we were apart from each other it meant we had had a fight. It was true! He loved entertaining guests for lunch or dinner. He was proud of how we had set up our house on Valença Street, and the apartment in Piedade, Jaboatão. Every item was bought and placed by the two of us, be it a flower or a piece of furniture, a utensil, or a picture. Our house was very beautiful!

Whenever he did not feel up to completing a task, he would sit nearby and watch me. So, preparing to return to home at the end of one of our trips, he would look skeptically at the luggage and at our purchases. "Nita, you are too optimistic. Do you think all this is going to fit in our suitcases? Wouldn't you rather buy one more?"

"Wait and you'll see."

I would always make everything fit. "You are a witch," he would exclaim. It is true that on more than one occasion I had to sit on the suitcases and have Paulo lock them.

If a repairman were to come to fix a doorknob, for example, or when my eldest son, Ricardo, would come to assemble our electronic acquisitions, Paulo would hang around on "solitary duty." But he could not even identify a screwdriver. Once on a Sunday, he kept going back and forth, up and down, following the installation of wires and special light bulbs my son had gotten him after seeing him writing by insufficient lighting in his office.

He would always accompany me shopping. He would take such pleasure in pointing out this or that lipstick or dress color! He would gladly serve as an intermediary between the salesclerk in stores and me, be it in Recife or London, Geneva or São Paulo. He would encourage me to buy things by saying, "I like it," or, "I don't like it," and, "it looks good on you," or, "it doesn't look good on you."

Once while in conversation with my former classmates at the College in Moema, São Paulo, he spoke about the pleasure he took in accompanying me on these shopping trips. Some of them rebuked, "Don't set a poor example! Now, our wives will want that we go shopping with them, as you do with Nita! For goodness sake, Paulo, don't spoil our wives!"

My husband took great care of me. He would protect me from harassment, even though I could take care of myself. Similarly, every night he would make a point of turning off the lamp. That was sacred to him. Therefore, many times he ended up falling asleep holding the switch, waiting for my return, even when I was out of the room for a short moment. When that happened, he would say, "You took so long..." The sentence would lose itself in his sleep, as he was again lulled by my presence. Paulo's desire to please this partner of his was most uncommon. A few days after we started dating, I asked him, "What do you use in your hair?"

"It's a gel. You don't like it?"

"In fact, I don't like hair that stiff and stuck to your neck. Why don't you leave it as free as you are, loose in the winds of freedom?"

"You are right, but you don't think it would look ridiculous?"

"No! That way your hair will complement your face and your beard. You will look handsome!"

He then let his hair grow and go free, just like himself, his ideas, and how he felt in his life with me. He still seemed to have a touch of doubt, "Nita, are you sure I look OK like this, with this long hair?"

"You remind me of Freud and Marx. More than airs of others, you are in the plenitude of your own self!"

A few days later, putting his right arm around me, he asked me to go into the bedroom with him. "I would like you to select my clothes. I would like you to remove from my closet anything you do not like!"

He was anxious to take one more step toward his "visual renewal." That afternoon, we went to a men's clothing store, and the salesclerk who helped us that day has kept in touch ever since. My husband took up the habit of dressing, not in luxury, but in clothing and shoes of a style that made apparent what he was intimately: a lover of aesthetics.

From that point on, he would look at himself in the full-length mirror in our room when we went out.

Smiling, he would step in front of me. I would provoke him by asking, "Enjoying what you see, huh, Dr. Paulo?"

He wouldn't respond yes or no. However, he stopped defining himself as "skinny, ugly, and angular."

Indeed, he had not been brought up for those chores that have erroneously been called "feminine" tasks. It was hard for him to put the wet towels in the right place, to close the closet doors, and to do other similar jobs. On the other hand, he was very disciplined and organized in his intellectual work. In the summer of 1996—97, the last one we spent together at our apartment in Piedade, he noted on index cards the duration of our daily walks along the beach, the same way he had done, long ago, with his reading notes. This habit indicated more than his organization. It revealed a certain discipline he wanted to develop for the sake of his health and his life. Unfortunately, too late.

Pranks

Paulo used to enjoy pulling pranks on certain people, but only on those able to understand his boyish ways. He pulled many on my daughter, Heliana. On the eve of his death, when he came out of the operating room where they had given him a catheter examination and an angioplasty, he said to her, "Would you believe that that son of a gun boyfriend of yours called the operating room, and when I told him that everything was all right and thanked him, he replied, 'I am actually calling for Heliana, not for you!'"

He told her this while holding her hand as his hospital bed was wheeled along the hallway toward his room.

In another instance, while Heliana was on her way back from a test for a new job, the company called my house to ask her to return immediately, as she had been selected for the job. But when my anxious daughter got home, Paulo told her flat out: "Heli, they called from the company to say you did not pass the tests."

I was sorry for my girl, who naturally displayed her discouragement. Happy with her reaction, Paulo could not stand his perversity any longer. "No way. It was you, you little devil, the chosen one!" he informed her.

When Dalvinha—an extraordinary woman who has worked for me since 1970 and who was with us at our Valença Street house—would stop by our offices to greet us, Paulo would salute her by saying, "Dalvinha, I read this story in *Le Mond*, a bit of news about you that really impressed me! It said that you…" Then he would make up some fact about her, or her daughter, or her little granddaughter. She would laugh happily, for she understood his prankishness as a show of his friendship.

On the day Paulo turned seventy-six, our last secretary, Lilian, came to visit us with her little son, Gabriel, then four months old. From then on, he would ask about the boy on a daily basis, "And how is the Portuguese sailor doing?" She would laugh, knowing that Paulo was referring to the little outfit the boy was wearing during his visit. I questioned him about that form of address, since Lilian might not like the "title" given to her son. The question then took a new form: "How's the admiral?" Gabriel was promoted and lost the Lusitanian nationality.

He was always joking around with our groundskeeper, Genildo, who was from the wilderness of Paraiba and whose features clearly likened him to the Dutch, who settled in those parts centuries ago, "Hey, Sweed! When I have a chance, I'll take you to Stockholm! With a new suit on, briefcase in hand, you'll walk along the street. I'll walk right behind you. I want to see all the foreign economists ask you about the stock market and witness your success with the blonds from there!"

One day, he took a cab in Cambridge in the United States. His English was still heavily accented. The driver, a college student working part-time, made conversation. "Sir, where are you from? Where were you born?"

"I am Brazilian even though I'm coming from Chile just now."

"Brazilian, huh? Well, I am studying a Brazilian author who lived in Chile. I understand that he is visiting here right now. His name is Paulo Freire."

Surprised, Paulo decided to pull a prank. "Fortunately, that did not cause us any trouble, but rather started a friendship," he later commented to me. He asked the driver, "Would you like to meet this professor?"

"But, of course. I would like that very much! Very, very much!"

"Can you come to dinner with us tomorrow at six o'clock?"

"I'd be glad to."

"We'll expect you tomorrow."

Everything was prepared. The young man arrived punctually. Conversations and drinks continued for more than an hour. Eventually, Paulo stood up and asked, "Shall we eat?"

"How about Professor Paulo Freire?"

He opened up his arms and a large smile, "Well, it's me!"

They hugged. The North American's sense of humor protected Paulo and provided him with a good friendship. "He became my friend, not a disciple. In fact, I do not have, nor do I want, followers! I want re-creators curious about what I created, with my epistemological curiosity! He became my friend," he would repeat.

Taken aback by the speed with which technology produces amazing innovations, even scary ones, Paulo used to joke that in case his father, who died in 1934, came back to life, "he would just greet him with happiness and tenderness and ask to go back to sleep immediately, so as not to be shocked by the changes in the world. Only on the second day would Paulo start the litany of new items, the new initiation rite to our times." In homeopathic doses he would tell the news as if in Jules Verne dreams. "Remember? You used to read me his books and the ones by Aldous Huxley. They are no longer children's stories and reveries. The admirable new world is reality!" He would say, "Dad, what I find the most amazing is that we can dial a phone number anywhere, and there is this contraption attached to it where you can put in a letter and the other person gets it on the other side, every single word of it down to the writer's handwriting, even before the paper is done flipping over before your eyes."

Fascinated by the fax machine, Paulo concluded that if his father "could accept that thing, he was apt to survive in this end of the millennium."

Jim

Jim was a beautiful and loyal Valença Street resident.
Along with Andra, he had many children. In his wisdom,
Paulo not only loved the couple, but cared for them,
especially Jim. He was forever observing them, learning
from them. He would recount these lessons all over the
world. Reflections on the animal world and human
creation. Because, you see, Jim and Andra were a couple of
German Shepherd dogs who guarded our house. Jim got
old, gained a lot of weight, and his heart weakened. One
evening, we were coming home from the launching of a
friend's book. We opened the door and Paulo went to let
Jim out of the kennel. He soon came back with a sad look.
"Nita, go see what happened to Jim. He seems to be in deep
sleep; he didn't respond. Go see what happened."

"Could he have died?"

"I don't know, please, go see."

I walked into the kennel and Jim was indeed dead. Andra kept vigil. She did not cry, didn't howl, but for months she seemed to still be in mourning, apathetic and lifeless.

The following morning Paulo said, "I will have the sidewalk in the backyard broken up, and a deep hole dug to bury Jim right here, near us."

"Why not bury him on the ranch in Itapevi?"

He accepted my suggestion and, minutes after, in thanks for the work, the loyalty, and the ability to give that is displayed by dogs, went with the driver and an old employee of the house to bury the dog on my ranch near São Paulo.

Paulo made himself more human by embracing his animal side, but also by understanding and loving animals. He exchanged loyalty with them.

The "Fallible" Alarm

With the increasing violence rate in the city of São Paulo, we decided to install an alarm system in the house on Valença Street. With the gadget on and the code entered, any window or door, if opened from the outside, would sound a siren and send an emergency signal to the security company's central operations, warning of imminent danger. Final adjustments were made. Certain that sleeping with worry was a thing of the past, we were, nonetheless, awakened by the siren at six in the morning. The phone rang, and I answered. It was the security company monitor, who asked, "This is the 'drugstore.' Who is there?" According to instructions we had received, we were to respond by stating that everything was in the peace of the Lord. The system, however, had broken down. The whole Swiss-made network of wires, sensors, broken-glass detectors, and central operations was fallible.

"Nita, this thing has gone crazy," Paulo stated.

"Completely," I responded.

The alarm siren continued to issue its grating noise. I got dressed, left the bedroom and saw several neighbors near our gate. After his shower "to finish waking up," Paulo joined the small crowd that had been bothered by the noise, expecting the arrival of a technician. All of a sudden, two small cars pulled up in front of our door. Three armed security personnel got out, in uniform, conscious of their responsibilities. "We are under company orders to go into the house and see what is really going on."

I rebuked, "What we need is a technician, not security guards. We don't have any trespassers, just a defective security system."

The head of the group insisted, "We have orders to go in and search the whole house for the family's own safety."

"Hold on; I am going to call your central operations, OK?" I asked.

I called them, following the identification procedure, and asked about the necessity of the "National Guard." They told me, "Madam, I have called your number three times saying, 'this is the drugstore, who is there?' A male voice kept responding, 'This is the number, but I don't want anything from the drugstore, as if I didn't have enough trouble with all that is going on here without being bothered by you people from the drugstore!'"

I broke into laughter. Paulo had never gotten used to dialogue codes, to number codes, to turning things on and off, and to closing or opening doors quickly. He forgot all about the "lessons" given by the security company; they had been too much trouble for his way of being. I went back to the crowd. Paulo asked, "What is going on?"

"What did you say when they called from the 'drugstore'?"

A bit calmer, he realized the misunderstanding he had caused. In his naughty-boy way, he confessed, "Oh! I got aggravated and told her to go to hell!"

The security men, with their cell phones, weapons, beepers, and codes, received their instructions and left apologetically. Baffled with all the disarray, the siren silenced by itself. Paulo said good-bye courteously, "Take care, thank you so much. I make all the trouble and you folks apologize. Nita, how is it that I should answer when they call from there?"

We embraced and went in for breakfast.

Seduction Secrets

In March of 1989, I went on my first trip with Paulo, to Fortaleza, in response to two invitations. One was for a gala evening with one thousand educators, where Mayor Luiza Fontenelle presented Paulo with the "Frei Tito" decoration. It was an emotional event.

The following morning, at the Federal University of Ceard, the large audience spilled into a backyard shaded by grand mango trees. The setting inspired Paulo. He delivered a beautiful, rigorous, scientific speech, in which he dedicated minutes on end to speaking about his love for me.

At the end of his talk, the small stage filled with people who, as always, plied him with questions. All of a sudden, two women, apparently older than me, whispered into my ear, "We would like to ask you a question!"

"Go ahead!"

I was proud, thinking that they had knowledge of my work in the history of education. But they responded, "Not here!" We went out of the auditorium, and, embarrassed, one of them asked, "What did you do, Madam, to catch such a fabulous, wonderful man?"

I quickly thought that that question, asked as it was in a malicious tone, through oblique gazes, suggested spells, covenants, rituals in water basins, candles to St. Anthony, visits to voodoo centers, blood sacrifices, or even tricks of seduction worthy of Eve's pursuit of Adam. They supposed "illicit practices" on my part, of the kind where men cannot choose but are rather captured in feminine traps. Faced with those suggestions, I answered, "Nothing! I did absolutely nothing…I am!"

"Epistemological" Doubts

In 1989 we went to Uruguay. During conversations and meetings, always together, we caressed each other and could not imagine that we were being observed. These were instinctive, natural gestures between Paulo and me. The years went by, and one day, when he came back from Campinas, he asked, "Do you remember your Uruguayan psychology students, who were always with us in Montevideo?"

"Yes, I remember them well."

"They asked to come here to our home to discuss some issues that are making them restless. They are now graduate students at Unicamp."

I agreed to the visit. A few days later, they arrived at our house on Valença Street. Questions and doubts were discussed, books from the library were consulted, photographs and smiles. I thought, "*They must be happy with the treatment of their epistemological doubts.*"

The four of us had lunch. Little by little they became more comfortable with me. Before coffee, Paulo left the room. The two exchanged glances and must have thought, "Now is the time!" One of them mustered the courage to tell me, "You know, we came here with a task."

"What task?"

"To verify if the Professor still caresses your thighs. Everyone at the university found that gesture to be…well…to be quite daring."

I laughed a great deal at those observers of our body language and their reaction. I asked, "Well, then? What have you observed?"

"That the two of you remain the same!"

"How wonderful that the years have not erased our passion and ardor for touching one another's bodies."

"We will report that back in our country!"

"You can go ahead!"

Paulo joined us. We conversed a bit longer. When the students left, he laughed a great deal upon learning the true mission that had been assigned them and that they had carried it out with such pleasure and friendliness.

Holding Hands

We were special dinner guests at the home of a college director in New York State. We were immediately received with friendly greetings and drinks. Light conversation, a full room, and many smiles. The hostess invited us all to help ourselves to dinner in the adjacent dining room.

While we were still selecting what we wanted to eat—vegetable salad, smoked ham, cheeses, fruits—the huge living room was rearranged. Paulo and I returned to the two armchairs where we had sat down when we arrived. The rest of the space was filled with auditorium style chairs, placed one behind another.

Paulo commented, "I thought I was going to escape a third conference today, but I guess I was wrong." While the School of Education faculty ate, questions were asked and were echoed from every part of the room. In the capitalist world there is no time to be wasted: any time is a good time to know and to gain. This group didn't even notice that. It was compulsive.

At one point, a serious and focused woman in her mid-forties stood up. In good observance of local custom, she asked, "Professor Freire, I would like to know how a man respected throughout the world, a famous educator..." She cleared her throat several times, and finally concluded her question in a nervous voice, "how can you be touching and caressing your wife's hand in public all night?"

There was a thundering silence! What a difficult question! "*How will Master Freire get out of this one?*" said the faces of the whole group of scholars, all arranged before us, petrified by the inquiry.

Paulo laughed and started by saying, "From your posture and that of your colleagues, who seemed to be holding their breaths while you asked the question, one would have the impression that I would not know the answer. But it is easy, my dear. First, you said 'your wife.' While I do not intend or am not able to make her my object, she is *my* wife, to the extent that I am *her* husband. I took her hand, my wife's hand, not that of any other: that would be too bold and disrespectful. Holding and caressing her hand feels right because she enjoys it and responds with the same tenderness that I want and enjoy. In addition, this does not interfere with my ability to reflect, but rather it deepens it. Could it be that responding here this evening, while holding Nita's hand, I seemed less capable to you than I did this afternoon at the School of Ed auditorium, where we sat apart from each other?"

The air cleared. It seemed as though many had been made a bit uneasy by the indiscreet question. For some hard-line feminists, this may have been some sort of censorship, also aimed at me; after all, leaving my hand available for a man to touch at will would be much too permissive for the wife of an educator, and of all educators, especially he who fought for the oppressed and against the objectification of the other for so many years. Paulo went on, "Thinking is not incompatible with feeling and pleasure. Rather, they complement each other. We should not be positivistic, but rather dialectic with our bodies as well!"

Applause, much applause! The atmosphere became amiable again. The conference was over. Nobody dared to ask new questions. The evening became happier, background music played again, and we went back to being the common human beings we are. Human beings who can think and eat in peace, while holding hands!

Green Eyes

At the closing of Lula's campaign for President at the end of 1989, we were on stage at a rally held in the Pacaembú stadium. Politicians, educators, and artists were assembled. I met several of them on that late afternoon, one filled with joy and the possibility that the Workers' Party could take the presidency.

At the event, a famous Brazilian popular music songwriter and I met for the first time. We looked at each other from a distance. He might have been thinking, "What must Paulo Freire's wife be like?" At the same time I came to realize, "He is just as good-looking live as he seems on TV." Paulo introduced us. We greeted each other. That was too much for my husband. He took me by the arm and took me to a corner, "That was a long handshake, and long gazes exchanged!"

"Not that long…"

"You were always saying that you would like to meet him. Are you happy now?"

I did not concede one millimeter in terms of my right to be happy to meet this songwriter. "So now I have met him. Excellent! And you, didn't you want to see him again?" Lula came on stage, speeches and more speeches were made, music filled the early evening's fresh air. And Paulo's bad mood continued. Many people offered to give us a ride. Long-faced, he would thank them and reply, "No, thank you, we have our car."

In reality, anticipating problems with parking, we had taken a cab. Paulo headed out, walking fast, deviating from his usually slow pace. I followed him. He would uselessly signal to cabs, all of which were taken. Eventually, we reached the huge hill that leads to Doutor Arnaldo Avenue. When we made it as far as the flower market, he invited me, but as if to exclude me, "I am taking a cab. Are you coming?"

"I don't think we need a cab anymore. We are a few meters from the house. But if you insist, sure I'll come along!"

I was happy with the resounding success created by my husband's imagination. On that day his tantrums, exploding through all his pores, mattered very little to me.

We went into the house; he kept quiet. He went to take a shower to wash off the sweat worked up by the uphill climb. A few minutes later, my daughter, Heliana, and some friends arrived, "We're so jealous! We saw you from a distance talking to…"

"Girls, don't say anything; don't speak anybody's name!"

I whispered to them what had taken place. Paulo walked back and forth, head down. Bia, one of the girls, whispered in my ear, "My goodness, I never thought I would witness such a thing. Paulo Freire is jealous!"

"More than that—he is having a jealousy attack."

Some time later, we went to sleep in silence. The following day, he brought me a bunch of red roses and this love note, which I will always keep with me:

Nita,

In the midst of a meeting, I find it hard to work. I can only think about you, your smile, your patience, your beauty, your humility. I never thought I could love this way, again this way, as I love you, crazily so, juvenilely so, daringly so, fearfully so, jealously so.

Is it possible to love so jealously?

Yes. It is possible because I love you completely; I ardently love you. Because you fascinate me, inebriate me, by night as well as by day. Because you gave me direction when I had lost my address, because you brought me life when I wilted away, because you gave meaning to my meaninglessness. I love you jealously because it doesn't matter why. But if you must know, I'll tell you: It's because I love you, madly love you. "No más."

Paulo

To this day I lose my breath just remembering that.

The First "Honorary"

I remember the minutes before the awarding of Paulo's first honorary degree, offered by the Open University of London. It was very solemn in the waiting room. A corpulent, crabby-looking sexagenarian who was receiving the same title asked Paulo, looking down on him, "How many doctoral degrees does the gentleman have?"

"Well, I am Doctor in History and Philosophy of Education by the University of Recife, and now this one today. It will be my first, perhaps my only, honorary degree."

"University of Recife? Where is that?"

Paulo warded off the other's arrogance with cordiality, "In the Brazilian Northeast. Recife is my hometown."

"I don't know the place. You know, this is my third honorary! Third!"

As he proclaimed that, he put on the proper attire for the academic festivities. Paulo, reacting with simplicity, stated, "Congratulations."

Whenever he was reminded of this event, Paulo would ask me laughingly, "Hey, Nita, now I have more than thirty titles, is that right? Do you think he got past that third one?"

"Who knows? In modesty or geography, he will certainly not have gotten any."

"I never got any awards for modesty. But it would be crazy to find out that he was honored for being modest. It would be too much!"

The Clouds

Gazing at the sky was one of the many childhood habits Paulo did not lose, but rather maintained into adulthood. To him, it was a profound moment of contact with nature. The sky attracted him because of its infinite, mysterious, and unexplainable dimension. "When I was a kid, I was made to believe that everything comes from the sky: God, good and evil, the rain, the sun, the moon, and the guardian angels."

He would contemplate the sky and become elevated by its color and its vastness. He enjoyed the bright sun, luminous and generous; and the moon, which sparked in him the desire to sing. Since he had not sung in many years, he would whistle a greeting to the moon and to me as well. But above all he loved the clouds, in constant motion, whose shape he enjoyed "interpreting" for me. "Do you see a woman's face over there? The Christ over there? A gentle walking lamb just ahead? I see men and women walking away, disappearing!"

I would respond to his observations and confirm his reveries, and that gave him immense joy.

"Yes, I see!"

Or other times, to his disappointment, "I don't see that, Paulo."

"Don't you take pleasure in seeing these intriguing whims of nature?"

"Yes, somewhat. Not as much as you!"

"Incredible. Do you see how the figure becomes more beautiful as it moves across the sun?"

An amateur environmentalist, he never tired from contemplating and realizing the intriguing art of cloud movement. As he himself engaged in his creativity exercise, the beautiful and harmonious flow of his whole being became reflected in the mirror of clouds.

Fear of Flying

"I am afraid of flying," he would admit openly. The emotion was manifested in many ways. He would always get to the airport so far ahead of the set time that we would get tired from waiting for our flight. I remember other more intensely emotional responses. We were traveling from Rome to São Paulo when the airplane went into some turbulence. The feeling was one of flying on a sheet of paper that was dancing in the wind. He was sitting in the aisle seat and I sat by the window. Once through the roller coaster, back and forth, up and down, he asked me, "Could you ask this attendant who is coming over there if…"

"… if the airplane is going to go down?" I completed.

"What a tasteless joke!"

I had tried to make light of the situation to ease up our tension, without much success. Then I responded, "Given that I don't speak Italian and am farther away, what else could I ask her if not about preparations for a disaster?"

"It is not funny! Don't joke about something like that."

Another time, we were boarding a flight in São Paulo, headed for Paris with a stop-over and change of planes in Rio. As usual at times like this, Paulo sat quietly, holding and caressing my hands. As we taxied down the runway for takeoff, he suddenly said, "I am in terrible pain!"

"Where does it hurt?" I asked.

The turbines roared loudly at the top of the runway, thundering away into take-off. I repeated the question anxiously, thinking about asking the flight attendants nearby for help, "Where does it hurt? I will ask to stop the plane."

"No! Don't do that… it's going away."

The sound of the turbines increased to a thunderous blast. More deafening than Alberto Santos-Dumont[1] would ever have withstood. Still anxious, I insisted, "I'm going to ask them to stop the take off!"

"No, don't do that. The pain is gone."

---

[1] Brazilian aviation pioneer, deemed the father of aviation by his countrymen.

"Is that the truth?"

"Yes, it is. Calm down!"

The giant settled into the sky, providing a pleasurable feeling of freedom. Calmer, Paulo resumed conversing with me.

Dignity in the Air

We did not know why on earth they had thrown us on a flight between Philadelphia and New York, after a few days of work in Villanova. After all, it's only a two-hour trip by train. We checked in and only after an hour did I realize that our boarding passes indicated seats 6A and 6F. I went back to the airline counter and received the laconic answer, "These seats are together. No need to change them."

I went back to Paulo and informed him that we were going to travel together, as always. It still took a long time until they called us for boarding. We went down a huge stairway and took a bus that snaked around the airplanes on the runway. Amidst laughs and clapping, three young men and two young women started singing a country song. At last, we stopped in front of the plane. Plane? Nervously, I asked, "Are we flying on this contraption?"

"Yes, we are!"

"Not me, please!"

The ultra-narrow steps seemed like they were going to fly off in the wind. At the top, the flight attendant, who was also the co-pilot, showed up, half bent, half standing. He straightened up, put on a navy blue jacket with golden buttons, and invited us onto the aircraft. The first to board, with great difficulty, was an extremely overweight gentleman. Suddenly, I froze, "Paulo, did you notice that the propeller is on top? I had only seen one other model like this, in the '70s, when my kids were little and used to buy miniature airplane models to assemble!"

"Take it easy, Nita. If they are using this equipment, it will be good enough to get us to New York. It's near; it won't take long."

"Take long! Will it make it? I don't think we should board."

The young folks kept singing. Although displeased, I boarded. I complained about having to bend down too much both to get through the door and to walk along the aisle in the "aircraft." We managed to sit, one on either side. I prayed the rosary. "There isn't even a bathroom, and I wasn't feeling well yesterday. What if I need to go?"

"You won't need to, Nita. Calm down."

We fastened our seat belts, the thing's engine made noise, and started to move about the runway as if it were an enormous motorcycle. As for the overweight guy, poor man, parts of him fell out of the seat and spilled over into the aisle. I didn't think it was funny. To my great annoyance, the young crowd kept on singing. To make matters even worse, a storm hit. We took off and the airplane gallantly pierced through the torrent, I must admit. After those minutes of terror, Paulo spoke: "I was terrified as well. I had to control myself because I have never seen you afraid of flying."

He closed his eyes for a few moments, relaxed, and asked, "Tell me, Nita, have you ever flown with so much dignity? It soars high, with great dignity, so sovereign in the air."

"I much prefer the dignity of a Boeing or an Airbus."

Shortly after, we took a breath of relief. The tiny thing landed smoothly. We survived, as incredible as it might seem!

The young group sang, more enthusiastically than before, the song "New York, New York!"

"I Was Born without a Compass"

"I was born without a compass!" was Paulo's constant good-humored statement. In fact, even after staying at a hotel for several days, he never knew, when leaving his room, whether the elevator was to the right or to the left. He would be happy whenever he recognized any avenue in São Paulo (usually Paulista Avenue and a few others we drove through more frequently).

One day in Paris, a Peruvian couple who had settled there in exile invited us for dinner. A bit tense, they argued about the best itinerary, what subway station to get off at, going this way or that way.

"This kind of argument won't bother us, Nita. I will follow your direction strictly. I never know where to go! I was born without a compass!"

Paulo used and abused the right to get lost or to wait for my lead when it came to itineraries. Once, I had a hard time believing he had gotten lost. We were at Loyola University in California, staying in a small apartment for visiting professors. Every morning we would go to a seminar and then have lunch, either at the university or at some restaurant in town. After ten days, I started to miss my housewife routine. I told him, "Today I will stay home to take care of the housecleaning; I want to put our clothes in order and make the rice and beans that you like."

"How am I going to get to the seminar room?"

I pointed out his route from the apartment balcony. "You go out of our building, go forward, cross that flower garden, and head for that building with all the windows. Right there, do you see?"

"I know. Then, what do I do?"

"That is where the meeting is. To get to the room, follow the hallway to the left."

"It's easy to go without you; but harder to be without you."

He kissed me and left. I rolled up my sleeves. Beans soaking, shirts in soapy water, broom in hand. All of a sudden, the doorbell rang. It was him.

"What happened?"

"I got lost! I simply got lost. I had to ask the driver of the little Jeep that buzzes around the campus to bring me back. I walked for an hour!"

"I can't believe it!"

"It is true, Nita. Take me over there! I can't miss this engagement, and it's no use trying to get there on my own."

It was no joke. I got dressed quickly, turned off the stove, and went with him. A few minutes later, some twenty voices were asking what had happened, interrupting the group work initiated by monitors, given the master's delay.

I wonder if anyone believed our explanation? Perhaps. But it was inconceivable to them that such a brilliant intelligence was allied to a head "without a compass."

Lost on a Cold Afternoon

After a nine-hour flight from São Paulo, we arrived in New York. The year was 1992. After waiting for some time, we went on to Washington, DC, where a young female OAS (the Organization of American States) employee waited for us. She was very attractive, friendly, and she spoke Portuguese. Soon we got to our hotel. We went up to our room, then quickly went out with the young lady to get lunch. The hotel was across from a square, and we had lunch at a wonderful restaurant. Both the restaurant and the square had Italian names. This was the only sense I had of where we were staying.

After we ate, I asked Paulo if we could go shopping for a brush and a comb, both of which I had forgotten to bring. The three of us walked until we found a store.

Suddenly, the American said, "It's three o'clock, and the honoree from Jamaica arrives in ten minutes. I'm sorry, but I am in charge of picking him up, so I need to get the car. We'll meet again tonight!"

Before she ran off, I just had time to ask how to get back to the hotel.

"Two blocks ahead…take a left…three more blocks on the right."

I finished my shopping and paid at the register. Then my doubts began concerning that business of going ahead, left, and right. To make things worse, the store was on a corner, and I could not remember which door we had come in through. We tried to retrace our steps in the store. But we were not very successful. Tired from the trip and from the walk, we asked ourselves what to do. Worse yet, we didn't even know the name of the hotel! The cold November wind started to get to us. We thought of stopping a police car and asking for some advice. We decided to take a cab and go to the OAS office. But the driver did not make things easier when he stated, "Without an address, I cannot take you there!"

We almost begged and he ended up acquiescing. The car cruised through streets and avenues. All of a sudden, in the late afternoon twilight, I spotted a building with a huge golden sign that contained the so-sought-after acronym "OAS." Paulo got out to talk to the porter, but he demanded a security badge. Paulo explained that he was not an employee of the organization but rather an honoree. "I am invited here. Tomorrow, I will be receiving the Andrés Bello Award for educators." Nothing, not a thing, could convince the corpulent porter, backed up by two, no-less-robust armed guards. Defeated by obedience to the rules and by the evident disadvantage, Paulo asked, "Could you, then, call someone who might help me?"

Down came an entire rescue team, including the guide who had left us at the store. Livid at the situation, she took us to the hotel. We soon regained our calm. One thing is for sure: Hansel and Gretel were right to mark their way back with pebbles.

"Cajá" Juice

I always joked with Paulo, saying that when he left Brazil for exile in 1964, he had probably made an oath upon the Bible to never lose his Pernambucan[1] roots, but that he had exaggerated the dose when it came to our foods.

This oath was adhered to throughout nearly sixteen years in exile in its most profound dietary sectarianism. Ever since childhood, Paulo had been a picky eater. In Chile, he added *loucos* and the local wines to his menu. In Europe, he further developed his tastes for wines, especially those from Spain, Portugal, and Greece. He knew them well and enjoyed them a great deal. He used

---

[1] Pernambuco is a state in Northeast Brazil; Recife is its capital.

to savor them as a man open to the new, which he was in *almost* everything, since new foods were excluded from this openness. I used to tell him, "You are more than a man of your time. You are a visionary. But when it comes to food, you are stuck in time and space, in 1930, in Recife." He would agree with me.

In the last ten years of his life, during trips abroad, he obstinately searched for beans and feijoada,[2] or other Brazilian dishes. Of course, he almost never found them. Aggravated, he would then demonstrate his dissatisfaction with the food offered by showing the new holes he had made on his belt. I would joke about it, "Someday I will have a little statue made of beans, and an inscription will read: *To Paulo Freire, deserving of the FEIJÃO, BEANS, FRIJOLES.*"

Jokes about his dietary habits would circulate among his friends in exile. Nonetheless, he would still not give up his standards. Only toward the end of his life did he become more flexible about his dietary preferences.

Berta and Darcy Ribeiro told me that once in Chile, inattentive and unfamiliar with Spanish, he got off a bus while it was still moving because he read a sign in the window of a fruit-juice shop that said "caja." He thought it meant the juice from cajá, a little fruit that gives off a

---

2   Feijoada is the national dish of Brazil, consisting of beans, pork, and vegetables.

wonderful smell, and whose juice is used to make a drink of surprising flavor. That is why he committed such a dangerous and thoughtless act.

He frantically requested from the counter attendant "a large glass of the cajá drink, with ice." Anxiously, he anticipated the pleasure of savoring the God-blessed juice. Confused, the Chilean behind the counter could not understand his odd request.

Then, Paulo suddenly realized that the sign indicated the area—the cash register—where people could pay for the different juices available: *naranjas, duraznos, ciruelas*[3]*... but not cajá, or mangaba, pitanga, graviola!*[4]

He told his fellow exiles about the incident, to share his disappointment, but contrary to what he expected, they would not give him any peace. The misunderstanding gave rise to teasing, which he did not appreciate. He would turn serious whenever he was reminded of his mistake. He learned to control his gustatory impulses, but not without suffering and longing for the smells and tastes of the Recife he so loved.

---

[3]   Juices commonly sold in Chile

[4]   Juices commonly sold in Brazil

A Stew of the Gods

We were planning to host an Argentinian couple. I had a wonderful Brazilian stew made. At lunchtime[1], he arrived by himself, for she had stayed in Buenos Aires on business. Our cook, Helena, came out and placed the carefully prepared specialty on the table. The white table cloth had been starched by Dalvinha, and the silverware, plates, and glasses were set.

There came a platter with green, white, and yellow vegetables lovingly arranged. Another dish contained various types of meats: sirloin, ribs, tenderloin, stew meat, different sausages, bacon, and corned beef. A terrine

---

[1]   In mainstream Brazil, lunch is often the largest and most important meal of the day.

contained the *pirão*.[2] The aroma was undescribable. The inebriating steam came up as if from the food of the gods.

We took our places at the table, and Paulo described the banquet with the sophistication of someone who speaks of his lovers. Our guest came up with a half-baked excuse, "I don't usually have large meals during the day." *"Why, then, did he accept an invitation for lunch?"* I thought. He snuck a peek at the platters, got up, and placed half a potato on his plate. Seconds later he forked up, even more quickly, a tiny piece of meat.

Paulo and I feasted by ourselves. Our friend limited himself to the two small excursions to the buffet. He had none of the fruit juices: cashew fruit, passion fruit, cajá, and graviola,[3] nor the fruit desserts, guava, banana, and jaca.[4] When our guest had left, Paulo repeated in frustration, "How terrible! What a terrible thing to do!"

I was surprised. I had never heard Paulo speak of other people's conduct, especially so harshly. All of a sudden, as if enlightened, he remarked, "Well, would you believe it, I did the same thing throughout the world during all these decades of travel?" And he justified the unexpected

---

[2] A typical starchy accompaniment to stewed meats or fish made with cassava meal and the stew broth.

[3] A typical Brazilian fruit.

[4] A popular fruit that was brought from India to Brazil by Jesuit preists.

confession, "I had never realized, as I did today, that food is the greatest cultural expression of a people! Today I witnessed it firsthand, the humiliation to which I have subjected so many people throughout the world by refusing to eat their most valued dishes."

From then on, he became more discreet in his refusal to eat certain dishes. But he never forgot our friend's repulsion toward "the most delicious dish in the world."

Tipping in Strasbourg

In August 1988, we were in Holland when we decided to go on to Switzerland by car. It was a tiresome trip, given the distance and the discomfort of the automobile, too small for the two of us plus another couple. It rained a lot and traffic was heavy. Amidst mountains, valleys, and rivers, we passed through Germany. At dusk, we stopped in the French town of Strasbourg for dinner.

The rain stopped. We visited the cathedral that unabashedly displayed the greatness of the human imagination. Imposing and majestic, it welcomed tourists from the world over as well as local believers.

We went for a quick walking tour of that beautiful city to stretch our legs and to give our pained bodies, compressed during so many hours of traveling, some relief. We picked a pleasant little restaurant for dinner. An open lanai and climbing plants in bloom created a cozy atmosphere. The table was well set: red-and-white plaid tablecloth, glasses, silverware, and napkins. There was a simply luxury to the place. "*Eating in France, how delicious!*" I thought.

Good gourmets that we were, we each chose, in the French manner, appetizer, entree, dessert, and beverage. The prices were moderate, and we were famished.

The restaurant had been full, and we had waited more than forty minutes for a table. We started to delight ourselves with the food, and each of us would let out an occasional "Ah!" of joy. After eating three escargots, I tried in vain to use the proper utensils to capture the remaining mollusks on my plate. Nine of the snail shells were empty. We complained to the waitress, a middle-aged woman with plenty of wrinkles, who share our indignation. "In ten minutes, I'll bring the escargots—all the ones the chef cheated you out of!"

She served the other dishes, apologizing for the inconvenience. Paulo appreciated her interest in serving me to my satisfaction. Ultimately, we ate well, in spite of the fact that my dishes were served out of order. The check came. Paulo gave his commentary, "Very reasonable for an abundant and tasteful meal…excellent wine!" He broke out his old wallet and paid cash, the price plus a 40% tip for the waitress. I asked if he didn't think that was a bit too much. He replied, "It isn't. Have you ever seen greater efficiency and friendliness than that displayed by this woman? She deserves to be well compensated."

"Where in the world are tips this high?"

"See, Nita, I was born naked and have all I have. She does deserve it! That's how it'll be."

As we left, we sought out our waitress to say good-bye. A fellow waiter informed, "She had to leave early." The suspicion hovered in the air that hers might have been a strategic exit, designed to preclude our ultimately regretting such great generosity.

"Paella" in Tokyo

We were on our first trip to Japan, in August 1989. Fascinating! We visited Osaka, Nara, Kyoto, Hiroshima, Aomari, and Tokyo. Palaces, gardens, statues of Buddha, temples, tea rituals, dances, Sumo wrestling, the bullet train, Mount Fuji, everything that Japan had to offer us, plus a full-time guide.

The colors, clothes, customs, and the hospitality dazzled us, as well as Japan's people's efficiency. "Being a guest in this country is the best thing in the world!" we would say.

Paulo would compare this Japan with the country in his dreams. He was reminded of the childhood fantasy about digging a tunnel from Recife to the other side of the world; a very different trip from the one we took around the globe.

However, two things were not going well. At bedtime, there we lay with our eyes wide open; during the day, our frustrating need for sleep required an extra dose of energy. The mismatching of our social and biological clocks was a nightmare for us. The other thing was the food, although this was only Paulo's problem. Personally, I was delighted with Japanese sushi.

At the end of the trip, in Tokyo, we gave our guide some time off to spend with his family. In our hotel room, while showing off his loose pants and belt, which already requiring at least three more holes, Paulo presented me with an ominous invitation, "Let's go out to eat. But I must warn you that if I do not find what I want, I will be upset!"

"It is very simple. Let us not leave. This way no one will get aggravated, only hungry," I said.

"I can't take it any longer. I want to get away from these watery broths with nothing in them. We still have two months until we return to Brazil. I need to eat!"

We went out, although without much hope. Because we were without our guide, I made a point of writing down all the information about the way back: hotel name, this sign, that tree. So we walked about with no fear of getting lost in this gigantic city without street names. As we turned the corner of an avenue, I was able to read, as it flashed in red neon, a familiar name. "Paulo, look at that.

Just past the Coca-Cola sign there is another that you will love!"

"I see nothing I am able to read, only Japanese characters."

All of a sudden, he smiled. He had made out the sign of his deliverance from hunger and frustration: "España." We marched over there.

"Nita, how does one go into this restaurant?"

"I don't know. Let's keep looking!"

After a long search, we found a narrow hallway that led to an elevator. We took it up to the sixth floor. A waiter greeted us, "*Buenas noches!*"

"A God-blessed salute," Paulo whispered. We had hardly sat at the table when Paulo ordered hurriedly, "A large *paella* and a bottle of Rioja!"

While sipping wine, we waited for the blackened baking pan. We talked with all the people who worked there—happy Spaniards who earned enough to visit their homeland annually and also to save some money. A small serving arrived, and we glanced at each other. "Small isn't it? Shall we order another?"

"Yes, let's do that, Paulo; the 'large' is not enough for two people."

Our waiter returned with a second serving of rice in saffron with shrimp, clams, other shellfish and mollusks. green peas, tomatoes, and peppers. Steaming, aromatic, and attractive it was, but I still think it wasn't all that good.

However, he had been eating poorly at meals for the entire twelve days of that trip, except for the morning meal, identical to the American breakfast. Driven by intense hunger, he repeating during the meal, "The *best paella* in the world!"

The Silver Tray

On our second trip to Japan in July 1990, we went to an international event in the city of Osaka as representives of the mayor of the city of São Paulo, Luiza Erundina. At the end of a long meeting, hot and tired, we returned to the fantastic hotel where we were staying.

By pushing a button near the bed, we could open the curtains that covered the room's huge glass window. On one side, we could see recently erected buildings with immense glass panes mirroring the enlarged image of birds in flight and the frantic bustling of the streets. On the other side, we beheld an ancient imperial palace.

Returning to our room, I checked all of our belongings: watch, ring, and gold chain. Everything was where I had left it in the morning, on a beautiful, antique

Japanese platter placed on the dressing table, next to the bathroom.

On the round table in the living room there was a beautiful silver tray bearing fruit: cantaloupe, melon, peaches, apples, pears, and huge, purplish, delicious grapes. Accompanying it was a very thoughtful card. I said, "Look, we got a most beautiful silver tray and some lovely fruits. There is plenty to sustain us until the evening banquet."

"The gift is the fruit, which is quite expensive here and much appreciated. The tray belongs to the hotel!"

"I don't think so. How could a company of this import send only fruit to the representative from São Paulo? The gift must include both items!"

"No, Nita, the tray belongs to the hotel! Leave it there!"

We ate the fruit. Two days went by and the tray remained there undisturbed. I would gaze at it covetously, convinced that it was a gift. "This tray is ours! See, there it remains, sparkling clean, ready to go into our luggage!"

"No, Nita, the tray belongs to the hotel."

Already on the plane, when it was too late, I realized clearly that, moved by honesty, we had ended up being less than courteous. And we lost a beautiful silver tray!

"Jerimum" Soup

Our group was made up of seven Brazilians, and we were at a banquet hall in Osaka. The owner was a Japanese man who had lived in São Paulo, where he still owned a catering business. The white linen tablecloth on the table at which we were seated was impeccable, as was the silverware with gold detail on silver and the crystal. We anticipated an oriental banquet, worthy of one thousand and one nights. I saw from the menu that there would be eight courses. I just couldn't make out what we would be eating. The host promised, "It is a surprise, but I think you all will like it."

They began by serving a salad, accompanied by French white wine. Several impeccably dressed waiters would remove dishes on my right...serve on the left...bringing little warm rolls, little toasts, and wines.

Next, the waiters entered with beautiful blue-green seashells on small golden tripods and placed them in front of our plates. Paulo was mesmerized by the "bowl," into which a creamy, dark, reddish-yellow soup was poured.

"Nita, I think it is jerimum soup!"[1]

"It can't be! Jerimum in Japan?"

Behind our grand Japanese-silk upholstered chairs, bearing intricate dragon carvings, a *nordestina*[2] voice intervened in our conversation, "Yes, sir. It's jerimum soup."

"My goodness! You are Brazilian?"

"Yes, sir. I am, and I have known you since 1980 when you returned to Brazil. I always used to work Saturday lunch at a restaurant in Panamericana Square, in São Paulo. I recognized you the moment you came in. The chef confirmed it. Many people here know you."

Feeling more familiar with that description, Paulo was happy to recognize the waiter's features and recall events that had occurred in Brazil. He tried the soup, having a few

---

[1]   A soup made from a vegetable similar to pumpkin.

[2]   Elsewhere in the text, nordestino/a is translated as Northeastern, referring to the Brazilian Northeast region. In this instance, the term is left untranslated, for it carries stronger emotional, ethnic-cultural content not expressable by the English word.

spoonfuls. He was prompted to ask, "This soup is cold, but it is very good. But, tell me, will there be any dishes a *nordestino* will not eat?"

"No, Professor, everything will be according to your taste. I know you well when it comes to food, and I am positive you will appreciate everything, all of it!"

Paulo gluttonously finished his soup and confidently awaited the new course. We came to realize as the evening unfolded that not only the utensils and ceremonies but also the succession of dishes had all been made to our Brazilian taste. No wonder! Forty of our compatriots worked there, in the kitchen, serving meals in the dining room, dancing, playing music, and singing sambas for lonely Japanese men. Later I noticed that I was the only female spectator present.

Unwanted Privacy

We went to Cologne in October of 1990 as special guests of a variety of German governmental organizations. While preparing to get off of the airplane in Dusseldorf, a civilian, and four police officers appeared at the door. The flight attendant announced in English, "Would Mr. and Mrs. Paulo Freire please identify themselves!"

Startled, I could not imagine that these officials were meant to honor us but, rather, to arrest us or inform us of bad news from Brazil. We identified ourselves and were escorted off the plane by the group, who also helped us to retrieve our luggage. They put us in a luxury car and escorted us with motorcycles and sirens. The civilian was a professor who rode in the front seat of the car. We arrived at a luxurious hotel, where he showed us to our rooms. He asked in English, "Do you like the living room?"

"Beautiful, comfortable, huge!"

He opened a door and said, "This is Mrs. Freire's room!"

"Paulo, did he say that this room is just for me?" I whispered. "Could it be that I do not understand English any more?"

"That is not possible, Nita!"

The friendly and efficient professor opened another door and proudly indicated, "Professor Freire, this is your room!"

"Oh! Absolutely not! I married Nita so I could sleep in the same bed with her. I thank you but we do not require this second bedroom!"

The professor blushed. He was lost in the situation. He hesitated but, ultimately defeated, he simply replied, "However the professor wishes!"

"I wish to sleep together with Nita."

We had never stayed in such a luxurious suite with such huge spaces. There were two bathrooms, two king-size beds in "my room" where we stayed, a dressing room, many large and plush couches, and a dining-room table for six. In spite of all that, I think we snuggled up closer than ever to sleep, in just one bed, as if going against a common habit in the First World, that of couples sleeping in separate rooms to preserve each other's privacy. When my nephew Thomas, who was a doctoral student in

Germany, explained the reason for the double booking of rooms, my husband commented, "I want nothing to do with such privacy! Rather, I want more and more intimacy with my wife! And you with me, right, Nita?"

He smiled, pleased with my conspiratorial look.

Tripe
a la Port

We were in Lisbon on a Sunday in December of 1992. We talked about how some Portuguese, attracted to the European Union, were distant toward Brazilians. Paulo understood and justified this separation. As we left the hotel he said, "Nita, a little sightseeing and then lunch, OK? I am going to ask the porter where we can have tripe a la Port."

"Don't ask that! If the dish is called that, you have to look for it in the city of Port, don't you think?"

"Why? Lisbon does not serve dishes from Port? It is all Portugal!"

"But in Europe, each region has its typical dishes that other regions never dare prepare. You have lived around here and should know that."

He took to the reception desk. I kept my distance, fearing hearing what indeed I did, "Well, then, you'll have to go to Port. The name says where you should order such things; here we do not eat tripe!"

The irritable porter's tone of voice and heavy accent made Paulo a bit downcast. He came back, took my hand, and we went sightseeing. He was somewhat disappointed for not being able to eat the dish he so desired and by the rude manner in which he had been treated.

Years later, I attended the final part of his last curriculum class with the students in PUC-SP's Education Program. From there we went to the faculty lounge, to discuss the itinerary for an upcoming trip we were taking with a group of faculty and students to Portugal. We agreed that on May 24, 1997, we would land in Port so that Paulo could satisfy his desire to eat tripe a la Port, right there! With a knowing smile, he showed his joy at his friends' consideration.

This trip did not take place. Paulo passed away on May 2, taking with him this and other simple desires.

Grilled Cod

Coconut milk. This was the ingredient my husband loved to have in bacalhau, shrimp, soft crab, lobster, and even maxixe[1] dishes. I always preferred salted cod on the grill, topped with olive oil. That was how I ate it during my travels with Paulo, whether in a Portuguese friend's restaurant in Geneva, or other places in Brazil and around the world. When we could not find cod in coconut milk, he would invariably order pork, even though I tried to talk him into other dishes. A futile effort.

On a Lisbon summer evening in 1992, after enjoying the hillside streets and all the ancient houses with their

---

[1] Maxixe (pronounced *maashish*) is a common vegetable widely eaten in the Brazilian northeast.

centuries-old rooftops in Alfama, we went to dinner at a fado[2] house. Paulo enveloped me in his arms, enjoyed the wine accompanied by huge olives. He looked at me with warmth and listened to the fados, beautifully sung by women in traditional costumes. We anticipated our dinners. The waiter approached, "Sir, it will not be possible to fulfill your order…we are out of young pig."

"Paulo, don't think so much, take the opportunity. There is the finger of God in this. It is suggesting that you try the grilled cod."

"I'll have pork chops instead."

I reaffirmed my order, "For me, please, the grilled cod with all the works. I have waited twenty years to come back to Portugal to eat this dish again, as only you folks know how to prepare."

Half an hour later, the waiter brought back a small platter with three white poorly fried pork chops. Paulo looked at them with disgust. He begrudgingly ate two. Then came my cod dish, bathed in olive oil with potatoes and olives, giving off a delicious aroma. He asked, "Can I try it?"

"Absolutely! Do!"

He tried it, almost fearfully. Then he exclaimed, "There, Nita, I must hand it to you. This stuff is wonderful!

---

[2]   Traditional Portugeuse music.

So many years stubbornly insisting on cod in coconut milk. From this day forth, I am introducing grilled cod into my diet."

Spain and the Spaniards

We had two unforgettable trips to Spain. Unforgettable because of Spain itself, because of the work we carried out there, but above all because of incredible Spaniards: Ramón Flexa, Mercé Espanya, Jesus "Pato" Gomes, and Lídia Puigvert.

In July of 1994, Pato and Mercé met us at the Barcelona airport. Mercé was timidly young. Pato was joyful, talkative, loving of his country and its peoples, and expressed the feelings of all his friends. This was my first encounter with them.

Paulo and I learned to like the way Pato lived. We appreciated his life in a "communal apartment" with his friends, the manner in which he became totally impassioned over his women and devoted to them, and the generosity with which he hosted us, welcomed us, and shared his time with us.

The history of the friendship between Ramón and Pato dates back decades. As university students, they lived and studied in the Basque Country. Then came the Franco dictatorship, persecutions, and exile in Barcelona. In 1988, Paulo received an honorary degree from the University of Barcelona, and there were the two, along with Josep María, a friend who photographed the event.

The next day, Josep went to Pato and Ramón's house, and after some goofing around, he showed them the newspaper with the lottery results. Unbelievable! The ticket Josep had bought was the winning ticket for the top prize of the day! The equivalent of two million dollars!

They celebrated, celebrated, celebrated. Happiness aside, they asked themselves, "What should we do with so much money?" First, they bought a bigger apartment for the "great big family." Unbelievably, Josep gave Pato half of the prize.

For his part, Pato gave half of it to his ex-wife, then bought a publishing house and an Audi. There was money left over, so he invited several friends for a cruise in the Greek Islands, for as long as the money lasted, since the return tickets were paid for. His publishing house, El Roure, still exists today, proliferating and guaranteeing his living. In Pato's apartment, these friends live together with their wives and children in enviable harmony. His Audi is no longer a killer machine, but it took us to wonderful places in Spain.

❀ ❀ ❀

On that hot day, Pato and Mercé took us from the airport to the hotel. After a short rest, we took a tour of the city, and viewed the entire skyline, in which the Sacred Family Cathedral, Gaudí's majestic work, stood out. We had a memorable dinner at a restaurant in the old city. We ate all kinds of things: bread and tomatoes, various tapas, blackened rice made with squid dye, fish. Everything accompanied by *cava*.

Our work was interspersed with visits to museums, esplanades, and wonderful restaurants. We delighted ourselves with the food and our friends.

//

After we had finished our work, our friends offered us three days of rest in Empúrias, a locale in Costa Brava surrounded from above by the ruins of an ancient Greek city, and from below, along the coast, by a Roman town.

We had rented a car. Donaldo Macedo, who had come from Boston for the same conference in Barcelona, accompanied us. Shortly after they had gotten us settled in and had lunch with us, Pato and Lídia returned to Barcelona in the Audi.

We decided to explore the region. We walked to La Escala, a town that attracts tourists because of its specialty: anchovy in preserve with bread. We went by car to Perignon, in France, and to Rosas and Figueras, in Spain. In this small town, where Salvador Dalí was born, we visited a museum with a great many works by the famous Catalan, from the most exquisite to the most extravagant. In some, one could read the signature, Salvador Gala Dalí. Perhaps this was an explicit show of his passion for his wife, Gala.

Donaldo goaded Paulo by asking, "Paulo have you ever signed any of your work as 'Paulo Nita Freire'?"

"Not yet, Donaldo."

On the third day, following Pato's recommendation, we went to Cadaqués. It was a beautiful but frightening trip, with sharp curves and steep cliffs all along the road. I was at the wheel, Donaldo was in the back, and by my side, Paulo seemed like a radio announcer, "Goodness! Two cars completely wrecked down there, about one to two hundred meters. God, what a terrible precipice!"

He talked and talked, as if he could ward off the danger that surrounded and frightened us.

"Donaldo, can you see the car and truck wrecks? Wow! That one must have been loaded with animals: I can see horse and cow skeletons. Careful, Nita, don't go too fast; let the people who are honking go around us; let them pass."

"What do you mean, let them pass? Can you stop this mad narration right now?"

Finally, as if out of nowhere, there appeared, the old fishing village. Small, beautiful, and cozy, it had been "discovered" decades before by Dalí and Picasso. I believe by Gaudí as well. The town was a stronghold of relaxation and inspiration for these incredible artists.

Donaldo had been pale, absolutely frozen, during the ride. Born in Cape Verde, he was a North-American "on loan" to a university there, but a Brazilian in his soul. This all-weather friend asked Paulo, "You were terrified, weren't you?" Paulo confirmed his "absolutely legitimate fear." He gave a long speech, purging the excess adrenaline produced by the frightening sights.

"Paulo, I am no longer used to the Spanish roads. In the United States, there is no such thing, only very wide highways."

I spotted a police officer. I pulled over to ask him, "Officer, is there another road back by any chance?"

"No, madam. You will have to take the same road back to Empúrias."

We could only gulp and, right after lunch, took the way back even more fearfully and carefully. At night, the hotel operator called. I recognized Pato's voice. "Nita, I'm coming to meet you guys in Empúrias tomorrow."

"Oh, that is very kind of you, but it is not necessary. I know the way to the airport. We'll return the car there and fly on to Switzerland. Donaldo will go back to Boston."

"I am coming! Lídia, Mercé, and myself. Ramón won't be able to come."

At nine o'clock the three arrived. We departed almost immediately after. After an hour, Pato pulled the Audi onto a side road. He signaled for us to follow him. I obeyed. Sixty kilometers later, he turned into the parking lot of an old ranch that had been turned into a restaurant. It was an absolutely extraordinary place. The six of us exchanged glances among ourselves as if enchanted. The wonderful plot, masterminded by Pato, counted on the assistance of Mercé, with her habitual smile complemented by the movement of her delicate hands, and Lídia serene and happy. "This is our farewell present for the three of you who are leaving!"

Food of the Gods, wine of kings!

/ / /

Less than a year after those sweet adventures, we returned to Spain. The same group gathered again.

Chronicles of Love

We all worked in Valencia, Caslellón, and Alicante. Paulo, Donaldo, Ramón, and I attended conferences. Mercé, Lídia, and Pato promoted the books from his publishing house.

By night, we would dash to the *arrocirias*,[1] especially the one in Alicante, from which we could enjoy the view of the harbor, with hundreds of white boats owned by the rich and by local fishermen, completing the typical Mediterranean scenery.

I fondly remember the many meals that we enjoyed: paella, blackened rice, rice and shrimp, rice and chicken. We savored them so much that not one of us ever left a single grain from the huge servings.

The day we returned from Alicante to Barcelona, from where we would depart on business to other European cities, was unforgettable. We were in Pato's famous car. Paulo rode in front with him while Donaldo rode in back with his wife Lídia and myself. The tape deck alternated between songs and poetry by Juan Manuel Serrat, Rafael Alberti, Paco Ibanez, and…Pato.

Paulo repeated the verses filled with Iberian tragedy. The sights along the coast varied greatly: mountains, bays, beaches, and white houses. The atmosphere inside that automobile can't possibly be described. Some transcendental aura united us, one only enabled by the reunion of good

---

[1]   Restaurants that specialize in rice dishes.

friends cradled in the sensibility of these great troubadours of Spain.

Alberti's husky voice searching, in great suffering for a Spanish identity and for love, would be followed by Serrat's moving and beautiful voice singing the verses by Antonio Machado:

> *Walking are your footsteps*
> *the path and nothing more;*
> *walking, there's no path*
> *walking makes it path*
>
> *Walking makes the path*
> *and casting back one's sight*
> *one sees the trail one shall*
> *never go back to walk*
>
> *Walking no longer path*
> *not but ocean born star…*

After we completed a morning of work, Ramón and Lídia met us for lunch in the middle of the trip. The restaurant that we chose had an interesting history. Years before, a few rebels had gathered there to plot against the government. The tranquil street hid the impetuousness and the contentious spirit of these people. At one point,

Chronicles of Love

Pato expressed a rare concrete need in that lyrical-musical-revolutionary environment. "Paulo, I hope your next trip will be to receive one more honorary degree. You brought us luck that winter in 1988. We won the lottery after photographing and applauding you. The only thing is that my Audi won't withstand the trips yet to come!"

We did not return to Spain. We were preparing to go to Malaga, for another of Paulo's degree awards, when death took him.

I don't know how Pato's Audi might be doing. I met Ramón and Mercé at the V Confitea, a conference devoted to adult education, which paid a great memorial tribute to Paulo in Hamburg. Along with other great friends were Heinz-Peter Gehardt and his wife Fatima, who helped me during my first trip without Paulo. They accompanied me for the ten days that I was in Germany.

I don't know how it will feel to see the museums, the restaurants, the beaches, the cities, the troubadours and their songs without Paulo. I know that returning to Spain will imply a difficult and necessary reunion with all of these people, and that repeating the verse so many times sung in that car ("*we are touching the depths...we are following the depths*") will not have the same meaning. But I am sure that life will go on, and that we will continue to plumb the depths of our hearts with sincere friendships.

Cabidela Chicken

We were in San Diego, where my son Roberto lived. He is an excellent chef. Paulo loved to talk to him about his "responsible/adventurous" ways, always changing jobs located in different cities, yet always finding good employment. He loved Brazilian cuisine, which he would prepare for us. We were chatting animatedly one day when my husband interrupted the conversation by stating, "Roberto, let's go out looking for it."

"Looking for it? Looking for what?"

"A live chicken, so that you can prepare some *cabidela* chicken!"[1]

---

[1] A typical Brazilian disk, the sauce for which is thickened using the chicken's head

"For goodness sake, don't even think about that. If they find out we are going to kill a chicken at home, the three of us could end up in jail."

"Could it be? Let's take the car and do some research around the neighborhood. Who knows, some Mexican grocery store might sell live chickens."

I could picture the newspaper story more or less like this, "Paulo Freire, Brazilian educator, his wife, and his step-child were arrested for participating in satanic rituals, sacrificing animals, slashing their throats and drinking the blood…satiating truly perverse instincts, typical of Afro-Brazilian rituals!"

"Roberto, if we slaughter the chicken—incidentally, you will be the one to do this—it will be inside the apartment. Nobody will know what has taken place, and we will eat a wonderful meal!"

Roberto tried a final argument. "Paulo, what will we do with the feathers? Throw them in the garbage? They will be the proof of the crime, the proof that will do us in. It's too much of a risk!"

I watched the animated debate without saying anything. I saw Paulo sit down, defeated by facts that his gluttony did not allow him to understand. He had a small dinner and went to bed heartbroken. "These people don't know what they are missing out on. Ai! How can they forbid the making of a simple *cabidela* chicken?"

Chic

We were on our way to Europe, traveling in the refined first-class cabin of the most sophisticated Brazilian airline complete with champagne before take off. Pouches with toiletries, including a few little bottles with French perfume, were handed out. Having put on slippers, we sat reading newspapers and magazines our seats reclined. We relaxed as much as possible. During take-off, we held hands.

The flight was smooth. Flight attendants started serving drinks and finger foods—an odd term in that environment, filled with jewelry and French cuisine: smoked salmon, slices of foi gras, giant crab claws, and caviar. A magnificent dinner followed, served on trays with starched white towels, Noritake china, silver utensils, and crystal. The arrangement had everything, even a little vase with a red rose.

Coffee, liqueur, and Belgian chocolates were served at the end of the meal. After this ritual, Paulo, who did not value all this chic stuff, called the flight attendant. "Instead of scotch or brandy, why don't you serve some genuine Brazilian cachaça?[1] Those pale golden ones that come from Chapada Diamantina? Suggest that to your manager!"

The young woman smiled and replied, "I will bring you a suggestion card, sir. You can write directly to the person in charge of that."

He did, in fact, send in the card, but never received a reply.

---

[1]   A distilled liquor made from sugar cane.

The Constitution Allows It!

Paulo had told me a story in the living room of our house many times, and always with a twist of irony. Once, after all the hassles of checking out of a hotel, traveling on the congested Los Angeles freeways, and standing in a long check-in line, Paulo felt certain that he would have enough time to have lunch at the airport, thus avoiding airplane food. He sat at a table in one of the fast-food restaurants and asked the waitress for two eggs, over easy, and two pieces of toast.

The waitress informed him that they had stopped serving breakfast, since it was three o'clock in the afternoon. "We only serve snacks now," the young lady informed him pleasantly.

"Would you please ask your manager if the constitution of your country prohibits serving my order outside of the usual schedule?" he asked.

The teenager went to the boss's office. After a few minutes, she returned with a smile and the answer, "We checked in our constitution, and found no limits on eating eggs over easy on toast in the afternoon. Please wait while we prepare your order."

Soon, victorious with his legal argument, Paulo enjoyed one of his favorite meals, accompanied by the waitress's benevolent smile. Perhaps she was a college student who did this sort of work part-time. In any event, she was pleased to have been able to satisfy the strange customer while remaining a loyal citizen of her country. In the meantime, she went on serving the other tables the "allowed" dishes for that time of day: soft drinks, hamburgers, and French fries with ketchup.

The Dark Side
of the City of Light

The hotel where we used to stay in Paris was extremely small and modest. But it was near the United Nations Edicational Scientific Cultural Organization (UNESCO) headquarters, an organization Paulo did work for, and the woman who owned the hotel was most obliging. We stayed there often. I indulged myself by visiting and revisiting museums and art exhibits. Evenings belonged to us. Together, closely together, we frequented the Paris nightlife, from the Champs Élysées to a variety of nightclubs.

Everything was beautiful. It was a dream to spend a few days in this city that does so much good for the heart and to the soul. But, as always, there was Paulo's problem with the food. He never acquired a taste for French cuisine. One night, he asked me to find a restaurant that served paella. I located one nearby and called to get directions.

"Let's go, Paulo, everything is set. I know how to get there."

We got off at the Nation subway station. It was completely empty at 8:00 PM. We went up a stairway. Winded, we saw before us a huge, poorly lit square. We were accosted by three young men who demanded our money.

The youths were skinheads in black leather jackets, sporting intimidating Mohawk haircuts. My husband was not intimidated. In an unusual burst, he fired in French, "Get out of my wife's way!"

Frightened, I pleaded, "Paulo, for the love of God, give them the money!"

"Step out of my wife's way!"

Incredibly, the young men retreated and left us alone, safe and sound.

Paulo and I agreed that it would be ill-advised for us to continue on foot. I proposed that we take a cab back to the hotel.

"We will take a cab and find the restaurant, that's what we'll do!"

We spotted a taxi and climbed in. Five minutes later, it pulled over on a filthy street, in front of an awful looking place.

"Ai, Paulo, what a horrid place! I'm not getting out of this cab! Let's look for a better restaurant."

I will never understand why he insisted on going in, or why I agreed to go along with him. At the door, the heavy-set Spanish owner, Carmen, argued with her son. Sitting on a stool at one of the four tables in the restaurant, he was accompanied by another young man. The altercation dominated the atmosphere of the room.

I insisted on leaving.

Carmen approached. "What would you like?"

"Paella for two."

"For one! Count me out of this, Paulo."

After taking the time to throw her son and his friend out of the place, the woman opened the freezer and started to take out shrimp and fish. Everything was frozen.

After an hour, she placed the paella on the table. Paulo, a bit embarrassed, invited me to share in that "culinary wonder." I was angry but also very hungry, so I decided to eat.

"It is excellent, isn't it? Admit it."

"It is terrible!"

But it was not true: Would you believe that the paella was quite good? Having finished dinner and paid the check, Paulo asked courteously, "Madam, could you call a cab?"

"There are plenty on the street!"

Before leaving, I needed to use the restroom. He thought it was strange, but I insisted, for we wouldn't make it to the hotel in time. The fat woman pointed to a little "outhouse" in the backyard, filled with piles of old furniture, bottles, and wood boards. I opened the door to the room and realized the obvious.

"Paulo, there is no toilet or light!"

Holding the door half-open, he helped lessen my suffering and humiliation, the details of which are not necessary to describe.

We walked out of the restaurant, went up the street and onto an avenue. There wasn't a soul in sight, nor a cab. I was in a terrible mood and let Paulo know about it. I complained about everything; that night, Paris came undone. That was when he told me, "You have acquired quite bourgeois habits, haven't you?"

"Me bourgeois? Not that! I am simply a person with good taste!"

"Don't twist things around!"

"Could you, sir, tell me the difference between bourgeois and having good taste?"

"I don't know. I don't even know why we are fighting."

"Oh, you don't? Because we wasted an evening at a horrible, dangerous place, right in the middle of the Parisian summer!"

"Do you eat the food or the beautiful surroundings?"

"I like good food. If I am in Paris, French food; if I am in Bologna, Bolognese. But in a pleasant and clean environment. Beautiful surroundings and good food are not incompatible, rather they complement each other. I tend to prefer locations under blooming vines, with interesting people around, good service, first-rate *French* food. Preferably on the banks of the Seine."

"Ah! You have acquired…"

"I have acquired nothing here. Quite the contrary, I lost. I lost a moment that could have been wonderful."

No cab showed up. We walked back to the Nation station. He asked hesitantly, "Do we have to go back by subway?"

"Why not? I go everywhere in Paris by subway!"

"I'd rather go by car!"

Revenge: "Ah! Admit it, Paulo. You have acquired bourgeois habits…"

Mental Bureaucracy

Slowly and gently, Paulo read his speech, paragraph by paragraph, commenting on them, expanding, deepening them, and becoming more and more enthusiastic. All of a sudden, from a corner of the huge stage, a young, beautiful, well-dressed woman who was directing the proceedings stood up. Apparently, she was responsible for timing each speaker's presentation and calling on the next presenter. She would then hand to those who stepped down a well-wrapped box, with a yellow and blue ribbon, containing a memento of the event. The event in question was an international conference in Sweden, planned a year ahead of time.

Blown up on a huge screen, Paulo's image exhibited exuberant beauty, characteristic of him in those moments when he delivered speeches. The young host was already in position, holding a box—a bigger one, for he was the keynote speaker. She headed for center stage, where he spoke while sitting, turning the pages of his talk on a small bureau in front of him. She walked over, quite erect and elegant, until she touched the bureau. With her back to the audience, she gave him some signal. Paulo looked at her. From where I was seated, I could see he hadn't the slightest clue as to what was going on. He went on with the speech as if nothing were happening.

The young lady moved a bit closer to him. He faced her. He went on, still enthusiastic, although more contained. The image got bigger. I could see the two in a dimension that only technology can achieve. Paulo looked at her one more time. Finally, it dawned on him. He then asked the young woman, "This little package you want to give to me is my cue that my time is up and I should stop talking?"

She responded that it was.

Paulo reacted by continuing his talk. The young woman remained erect and immobile. While he talked, he would at times look at her, at times look at the audience. They had hired him to speak for forty-five minutes, but we had lost about thirty-five minutes since we had gotten lost in the hallways of the enormous building on the way from our room to the auditorium. Motivated by her intrusion, Paulo doubled his speaking time. He interrupted his reflections on "Educational Cities" and began to expand, alternately irate and critical, about the bureaucratization of minds.

"How can you all pay for first-class tickets, a five-star hotel, honoraria, and meals for both myself and Nita and not let me speak? You end up making time into an end to all things, rather than a means, which it should be! Is that right? Again I am faced with a situation where we in Brazil have much to teach you in the First World. By materializing time, serving it, you ended up bureaucratizing the mind! Bureaucratic minds do not think, do not feel!"

He took up the time allotted for a break and part of the next speaker's, a Volvo representative who followed him. The applause when he left the stage, carrying his box, and the comments during the following two days indicated that Paulo's "little" message had given people much to talk about and, above all, to think about.

Fourth of July

Brazil was playing the United States in the World Cup. We were in Barcelona, at the home of our dear friends Ramón, Mercé, and Pato. Donaldo Macedo joined us and, in spite of the fact that he was a naturalized American citizen, he did not dare confront our organized cheering, even though we would provoke him with comments every time his adopted country's team would lose the ball.

It was the Fourth of July, 1994, the American Independence Day. The *canarinhos*[1] were not playing well. Leonardo elbowed one of the U.S. attackers and was ejected.

---

[1] "Canaries"—an endearing term to refer to the Brazilian national team players, a reference to their yellow shirts.

I could hardly watch the game, as I was terribly preoccupied with a different problem. Our friends would say kind words to me, and Paulo would try to console me. "Take advantage of this World Cup game. Remember that I had my entire first paycheck stolen in Chile when I was in exile?"

"How could this happen in spite of all my Brazilian know-how on preventing petty theft; how could I let them take our passports, the airplane tickets, the hotel vouchers? It was lucky they did not take the money."

"It happens!"

Nothing, not even my friends' support could get the scene out of my head. It had happened on the way back from shopping that afternoon. Lost within myself, I was thinking about my own mishap while he continued the story, "The other exiled Brazilians even organized a collection so that my family and I could get through that month. I had on a suit jacket and an overcoat and they managed to take my wallet from the back pocket of my pants. They have surgeon's hands. Don't you worry; that's life!"

However, I kept asking myself how we were going to continue our trip. How about our entry visas for Paris and Prague? How about Paulo's so-dreamed-of meeting with Karel Kosik? How about the UNESCO work?

Our victory on the soccer field was no fun for me. The following day, Paulo, Donaldo, and Pato accompanied me to the department store where our things had been stolen in the hope that the items that the thieves felt had no value may have been thrown into the garbage. Unfortunately, nothing turned up. Paulo suggested that we go directly to the Brazilian consulate. As soon as we arrived there, the security guard informed us that all of our documents had just been returned to the consulate.

I let out a shout of happiness. My sense of humor returned. The Consul General and the first secretary enjoyed the visit with the "Master," and, remembering the game the day before, I realized that the Fourth of July is not only a North American day; it can be all of ours.

My Beloved Soccer

We watched the final 1994 World Cup game in Vevey, Switzerland. Paulo was anxious. In the morning we strolled around the city where Chaplin spent his last days, spotting the places where Brazilian and Italian fans would be. Houses sported national flags; there were four of ours that we could see and eight of theirs.

Since childhood, Paulo had liked soccer a great deal. He considered it a loving game. "For a goal to be scored, the cooperation of eleven players is necessary against the eleven opponents, in front of a large crowd. Soccer generates a festive atmosphere of great happiness—or invasive sadness—of cooperation, of giving, of harmonious action, only marred, unfortunately, by so many acts of violence practiced by players and fans."

Who can forget player Bebeto's celebratory gesture, pretending to rock his faraway newborn son, to whom he dedicated the goal he had just scored? Delicacy of gesture, paternal sensibility integrated into the love of soccer.

Paulo always used to tell me that back in the days of exile he was opposed to the notion that soccer served to blind the people to the perversities of the military dictatorship. He disagreed that the "good revolutionary" should not root and cheer during the 1970 World Cup in Mexico, in support of the Brazilian team because that would lend support to a regime associated with torture and opposed to popular aspirations, rights, and interests. Paulo would disagree.

"A revolution which, under the guise of serving the people, takes away from the people the right to like themselves, to cheer, and to be enthusiastic about soccer, is not worthy of the people. Soccer is the 'sport of the masses,' of the people who are made happy by it and who struggle for it, to cheer or to play. The antidictatorship fight is fought on various fronts, but not by sequestering the people's right to have soccer. It is a right, it is a passion, having to do with our culture, with our heritage: the fakes and maneuvers on the field are the savviness of our people lived through the bodies of those playing. Look how the people become deliriously happy with the fake-outs. They are beautiful, wonderful bodies in motion."

❀ ❀ ❀

Back in Vevey, I had prepared a succulent Pernambucan hot dog for the "half-time victory party." As appreciated as it is popular, this dish is always sold near soccer stadiums. French rolls are filled with ground beef, sautéed with garlic, onion, cilantro, scallions, and paprika, and topped with sliced tomato, onions, and green peppers. Paulo spoke up.

"We will celebrate as I used to do in the glorious days of my Santa Cruz back in the fifties and sixties, in Recife, with this genuine hot dog. This is the real thing, isn't it?"

We were quite concerned as we ate during half time. It didn't seem good for our team, although the score was tied. At the end of regulation play, the score remained an exasperating 0 to 0. Paulo got up, tense and angry.

"Pack your bags! Tomorrow we have to go back to Brazil."

"But the game isn't over!"

That tie in the hot, far off California afternoon seemed like an omen of Brazil's irreversible defeat. Anxiously, we suffered thousands of kilometers away from the stadium, on Lake Leman, where the heat was softened by the night.

"I don't want to eat anymore. I want to go back to Brazil!"

"There will be overtime play. Besides, you still have engagements in Europe!"

"I'm leaving the room. I don't want to see anyone trampling us."

Penalty kicks. Paulo stopped watching the little screen. Endless expectation. All of a sudden I yelled, "We won! Their top man missed the goal! Unbelievable! We are the champions!"

We watched the penalty kicks, the embracing and the crying of players, the tribute to Ayrton Senna. American television showed a festival of exploding Brazilian happiness. Paulo stopped sweating, the usual spark returned to his eyes, and his head went back to thinking. Prior to that moment, he was all emotion: intense, passionate, thoughtless.

"My anger is gone. I will sleep in peace; let us continue our trip. Anyway, even in light of defeat, I would have taken care of my responsibilities. But now my motivation to work is doubled. I am very happy. I really love our soccer."

The World Series

We arrived in Los Angeles on a clear, pleasant Sunday morning. A couple of friends who were professors awaited us. The husband, Peter, greeted us warmly, but expressed a concern.

"What a long trip for you! Would you like to rest a bit before lunch? I am a little uneasy about this, but today is the World Series, and my wife Kathleen is rooting for one of the teams."

"No, problem! We can have lunch earlier, and if Nita wants to, we can go to the game, the four of us," Paulo informed him.

We relaxed a little. Next, we faced the Los Angeles freeways to get to a Korean restaurant. Excellent food from a grill in the table. Everything was excellent, served in a wonderful style. We ate contentedly, paid, went to the restroom, and prepared for the sports adventure. And what an adventure! Kathleen parked amidst an ocean of cars. The game had already begun. She took from her purse four tickets to the game and we walked to the stadium. It was not packed and there was little cheering, at least not by any Brazilian standards. We had very good seats, and Paulo would convey to me his limited knowledge of baseball, recently acquired from Peter. I asked, "Paulo, what is happening on the field?"

"I simply do not understand the logic behind the game. I don't understand anything from Peter's explanations!"

So there we were, confused. By our side, the couple watched the game without showing any emotion. I observed the environment. The biggest "wave" session I have ever seen was in motion. Fans would leave to buy hot dogs and popcorn for the family.

Suddenly, the narrator of the game announced that the game would be interrupted so that emotions could cool off a bit.

"Cool what off, Paulo?"

"I remain unable to understand."

I could not believe what I saw and heard. Everybody got up and held hands, dancing to a mushy song. People would follow the rhythm, moving their bodies a bit to the right, a bit to the left. This lasted about five minutes. I whispered to my husband, "Can you imagine this type of a break at a Fla-Flu[1] or Corinthians-Palmeiras final in Brazil?"

He laughed just thinking about all of the foul language used by the fans. We sat watching the game for another two hours. We left before the game ended. Our friends accepted the fact with some sadness, "Oh, that is fine, we've seen enough."

"Jesus, Mary, and Joseph! Had it been my favorite team, I would have wanted to see the whole game," I thought. As luck, or bad luck, would have it, we were unable to find the car in the midst of that huge, packed parking lot. It was useless to look for it. We had to wait for everyone to leave. The evening cooled off the pleasant Californian day.

Kathleen apologized. As we waited, we became fatigued and hungry. As time went by, the cold began to turn uncomfortable. At last the lot was almost empty and we found Kathleen's little green car. The game was still going on. I said to Paulo, "In spite of not understanding anything about the game, I have learned a lesson today about many things: a city built for isolation, every inhabitant in his or her own car, far away shopping centers, and infernal freeways. It all leads to this: everybody comes to the stadium to see one another. It

---

[1] Two popluar soccer tams in Rio de Janeiro named Flamengo and Flumense.

must be like their beach. The game is not that important. The important thing is just to know that one's neighbor exists, even if one must meet him or her in gigantic stadiums."

Paulo agreed. "That's right. Today we saw what individualism can do to people thirsty for real communication and loving contact!"

Is a Scent Contagious?

Shortly after marrying Paulo, he and I were shopping in a clothing store. I rushed out of the fitting room in the shop, which was located in São Paulo. He asked me what was going on.

"A smell like body odor is in the air! In the clothes I was trying on!"

"And what does that have to do with your not wanting to try on another dress?"

"This stuff is contagious, Paulo! I catch smells very easily! I smelled that odor, got scared, and ran out. The stench is in the air!"

"Don't say that! How absurd of a reaction!"

From then on, he would always repeat to me laughing, "It doesn't look good to say that a scent is contagious." I would not concede an inch. "Stench is transmitted by airborne bacteria; you CAN catch it!"

Years later, we were in a cab in Paris. It was a humid and rainy night in the middle of the summer.

I opened the car window from time to time to breathe. We were going from the Quartier Latin to our hotel on Avenue Garibaldi. I had to purge myself of the terrible smell that came not only from the driver's armpits, but also from his whole body. "I have never experienced anything like it," we whispered to each other in Portuguese, being careful that the bearer of this scent, also a foreigner himself in France, would not understand us. In our hotel bathroom, Paulo kept calling me insistently.

"Nita! Nita! Nita! Come quick!"

"What is it? You made me worried!"

"Would you believe it? Scents are indeed contagious! Get rid of this jacket and shirt; don't even try to save them. Not even washing will get rid of this damn stench."

He took a long shower, washing himself repeatedly. After drying off, he kept smelling himself continuously, concerned over whether that undesirable aroma had stuck or not. Being mean, I asked, "So, is a scent contagious?"

He had to surrender to the evidence. After this incident, every time someone would tell us any story that seemed less than plausible, we would ask each other, "Is a scent contagious?"

"Yes!"

Our Last Trip

Our last trip was to the United States in April of 1997. We went to finalize his agreement to work at Harvard University. Before going to Massachusetts, we spent a few days in New York.

This trip was deeply engraved in my memory because of the presence of my sons, Roberto and Eduardo, Eduardo's wife Elsie, and their son André, then ten years old. We stayed at Roberto's house and he was worried about Paulo, especially about his dietary preferences. He would make us a Brazilian dish every night.

Dudu would always wrap his scarf around Paulo at the slightest indication that he might be cold. He showered him with attention holding him when we crossed streets, bringing him French and Spanish wines and Brazilian newspapers. Elsie would make sure that there were some delicious beans whenever we ate with them, and they worried about our comfort and rest.

Five years before, André had made my husband an object of his attention. On a cold morning in his hometown, he said to Paulo, while fondling his beard, "I know you are not my grandfather, that you married my grandma, Nita, after my granddad, Raul, had died. But, Paulo, I love you! I wish you were my granddad. I like your laughter and to play with your white beard!"

He enjoyed his adopted grandson's tender gestures and words. During this trip, in spite of the amazing cold, the boy was forever inviting us to go out, sometimes to a toy store, other times to a Chinese or Japanese restaurant. In a gentle voice, which so moved Paulo, he would ask about his little cousin Marina—the daughter of Ricardo and Márcia—who lives in Campinas and, despite the distance, was always present in our conversations. When she was five, she also had declared her love for my husband in her way, as she told him about a dream she had had the previous night. "I was sailing along the rainbow above the sea of Piety, with my grandma, Nita. In a tight embrace, we would go to so many beautiful places."

"And I didn't go?"

"Look, Paulo, you were not on my dream's rainbow, but if you want you can come with us! I will be happy if you come!"

After this intense family experience in New York, we went on to Boston and Cambridge. New moments of work and comfort with Jim Fraser and his wife and also with Donaldo Macedo, Lídia, and their son, Alejandro.

Paulo had chosen Donaldo as his assistant for the course he was going to teach at Harvard. The plans for the class had been made via fax and lengthy telephone conversations a long time before. The final details were taken care of in two workdays in New York. As for myself, I was terribly excited about taking a course to improve my English, about being able to visit my loved ones, and about having the opportunity to visit Canada. I would be studying, reading, and completing myself with Paulo. He already predicted, "We will be able to see people and things again. Remember when we went to New York together for the first time in June of 1988? For the first time in my life, I attended a Broadway show and a modern ballet performance! We will go to other events of your choice."

It was all dreams, work and leisure dreams. My husband vibrated with happiness just to think that he would go back to teaching at Harvard, live in Cambridge, and just let himself be in Harvard Square.

Chronicles of Love

"You know, Nita, I sat here at this cafe so many times after going through the aisles of that bookstore. I enjoyed watching the beautiful young ladies, with their mini-skirts, experimenting with the freedom earned in this country through the feminist struggle. I learned a great deal from these North American women! They awoke me to the gender problem."

He would take a sip from his coffee, look at the thick layer of snow accumulated after an unexpected storm, and he remembered that it had been in this aristocratic place that he had once had the terrible experience of having swallowed a fly while lecturing! He spoke about his fascination with New England and its people. Paulo turned to his new assistant, an old publishing partner, "Donaldo, my old friend, something tells me that I will write a lot here. It is my political duty. I still have much to say beyond this 'knowledge necessary to the educational practice,' and beyond *Pedagogical Letters,* now in progress."

These moments of happiness for the three of us are lodged in my memory; we could never have supposed that they would be the last of his existence.

"You know, Nita, yesterday Donaldo got me to thinking about some things to write about. The son of a gun made me feel that I can continue to make my contribution to current political thought."

My Life with Paulo Freire

We returned through New York. There, he insisted on getting me a bottle of Chanel No. 5, the perfume I had always wanted, but had always hesitated about accepting, in spite of his insistence. During that afternoon of shopping, he patiently remained sitting in an armchair in the store; he no longer stood between the fitting room and the salesclerk, as he had done nine years before. He felt tired, but he still expressed his preferences.

"This ensemble, yes! It was made for you. Get it! That other one I didn't like, it doesn't work for you!"

When we went to pay, the young woman at the cash register could not contain herself. "What a beautiful thing to see, sir, you helping your wife to choose these clothes. It is rare to see a husband like that!"

That I am sure about!

Paulo Meets Darcy

In the living room of our small apartment facing the ocean in Jaboatão dos Guararapes, we watched on TV a most beautiful interview with Darcy Ribeiro. His last. We knew he was near death, after having deceived the concrete image and the feared fact for decades, but it eventually comes to all of us. Thus, we listened to him attentively. His unique human figure, his immense capacity for loving people, his beauty even before imminent death, made him more alive than ever. The interviewer, Roberto D'Avila, knew that and knowingly gave him time so that he could show the greatness of his soul.

In the final part of the interview, Darcy spoke about his mother's death. She had gone calmly, full of faith, and closed her eyes certain of her encounter with the Lord. He spoke with healthy envy about that moment of profound faith lived by his mother and those who believe in eternal life. With bright eyes, Darcy said, "My body will become dust among others and will forever circulate in the cosmos. If there were a decree to give people faith, I would like one please. But such a decree does not exist…I wish I had been a man of faith, but I am not." We witnessed that man, so well known and loved by us, who did have a lot of faith. He had faith in the men and women of Brazil.

At that point, Paulo made a comment. "When I meet Darcy in heaven, he will tell me about the darn scare he experienced! And, with humility, something rare in him here on Earth, he will admit to me, 'You, Paulinho? My God! Look: God does exist; heaven exists; we are in it, Paulinho! We loved and worked so at His image and likeness…there is such a thing as eternal life! Praised be Lord! I did not become dust polluting the cosmos! I am here with you, in my mother's heaven, your mother's, all of ours!'"

Paulo stopped, was silent for a moment, and completed his thought. "Well, not me. I know that I will meet Darcy, as well as the men and women who have already departed and who I met and loved here. I will laugh; we will laugh again together. We will think together about Brazil and about those of you who might still be here. I will not be afraid because I believe in eternal life!"

This meeting took place, I am sure, after Paulo took me in his last embrace and then departed. It was the morning of May 2, 1997, at exactly 5:30 A.M.

To Those Who Helped Us To Be Happy

With what longing for Paulo have I written these chronicles! Truthful they were as they took place, truthful they are in my remembering these ten years during which I had the privilege of loving and being loved, of cooperating, of teaching and learning side by side with a loving man, as tender and sensitive as Paulo. The whole world knows about his intelligence, about his work, and about his devotion to the oppressed.

I have spoken here about the person who passionately lived every moment of his life. He would fight, argue, feel, discuss, love, and give all of himself. I speak about the man who avidly wanted, by his tenderness, by his loyal presence, to share all the moments of his life with me.

He knew how to fight for what he wanted intensely, tenderly, and seductively.

I wrote a large portion of this book, this testimony to our love, while sitting in the chair of our office in the apartment we put together, piece by piece, in Jaboatão dos Guararapes, in the glorious State of Pernambuco. This chair allowed me at times to write and at times to see the Piedade ocean, full of life, the beach filled with people in colorful clothes bathing in the generous *nordestino* sun or in the warm waters of that greenish-blue ocean.

I cry while remaking my life without Paulo, while remembering my life with Paulo. Tears, colors, the ocean, people: it all has to do with him, with our shared life. It all has to do with his way of existing. It all becomes amplified and moves me. Everything revolves around his presence, around his definitive and painful absence. Only Maria[1] is taking care of me now, as she took care of the two of us.

I could not fail to proclaim, as I finish this book, that the life we lived, intensely and deeply touched by love and passion, would not have been as plentiful had it not been for the presence of a few people, both living and dead, who are very dear to us.

---

[1] Nita's family housekeeper.

Dona Edeltrudes, or Dona Tudinha, Paulo's mother, for the manner in which she educated him and respected him, giving him freedom to be himself. For the way in which she battled for him, looking for a school so obstinately that she met my father, who gave him an education and her the possibility of being proud of her son for his extraordinary capacity to create and to think. His capacity to be human and to make himself the person that he was, came as the result of the totality of her care for him.

Aluísio, my father, with his tremendous goodness and generosity, for his understanding that education is a right of men and women. He offered Paulo the opportunity to complete his secondary studies in an era when the State of Pernambuco had only one high school.

Further, he offered him his first job, making him a teacher of Portuguese in his respected Oswaldo Cruz School. Thus, my father prepared him, formed him, and educated him for life, freely open to another. Without predicting it, he made it possible that one distant day Nita and Paulo would come to offer themselves to one another, to share a plentiful life.

My children, Ricardo, Eduardo, Roberto, and Heliana, who understood so well our entitlement to loving one another. For having respected, without reservation, my choice to remake my life. For having understood that loving a new partner does not mean forgetting the first.

For knowing that Raul will remain in me, as will Paulo, for my whole life. For having accepted a new marriage, and behaving respectfully, with dignity and maturity, toward Paulo and me.

I thank you, my children, for your love and solidarity, your sympathy, and the tenderness with which you treated Paulo during the ten years we lived together.

To all our friends, I would like to publicly say thank you so much for helping us to be happy again. Praised be you!

Studies in the Postmodern Theory of Education

General Editors
Joe L. Kincheloe & Shirley R. Steinberg

Counterpoints publishes the most compelling and imaginative books being written in education today. Grounded on the theoretical advances in criticalism, feminism, and postmodernism in the last two decades of the twentieth century, Counterpoints engages the meaning of these innovations in various forms of educational expression. Committed to the proposition that theoretical literature should be accessible to a variety of audiences, the series insists that its authors avoid esoteric and jargonistic languages that transform educational scholarship into an elite discourse for the initiated. Scholarly work matters only to the degree it affects consciousness and practice at multiple sites. Counterpoints' editorial policy is based on these principles and the ability of scholars to break new ground, to open new conversations, to go where educators have never gone before.

For additional information about this series or for the submission of manuscripts, please contact:

Joe L. Kincheloe & Shirley R. Steinberg
c/o Peter Lang Publishing, Inc.
275 Seventh Avenue, 28th floor
New York, New York 10001

To order other books in this series, please contact our Customer Service Department:

(800) 770-LANG (within the U.S.)
(212) 647-7706 (outside the U.S.)
(212) 647-7707 FAX

Or browse online by series:

www.peterlang.com